THE DH.

In a meeting with Samuel Bercholz, the president of Shambhala Publications, Ven. Chögyam Trungpa expressed his interest in publishing a series of 108 volumes, to be called the Dharma Ocean Series. "Dharma Ocean" is the translation of Chögyam Trungpa's Tibetan teaching name, *Chökyi Gyatso.* The Dharma Ocean Series consists primarily of edited transcripts of lectures and seminars given by Chögyam Trungpa during his seventeen years of teaching in North America. The goal of the series is to allow readers to encounter this rich array of teachings simply and directly rather than in an overly systematized or condensed form. At its completion, it will serve as the literary archive of the major works of this renowned Tibetan Buddhist teacher.

Series Editor: Judith L. Lief

The *Heart* of the *Buddha*

Chögyam Trungpa

Edited by Judith L. Lief

Shambhala · *Boston & London* · *1991*

SHAMBHALA PUBLICATIONS, INC.
Horticultural Hall
300 Massachusetts Avenue
Boston, Massachusetts 02115
www.shambhala.com

13   12   11   10   9   8   7

Printed in the United States of America

♾ This edition is printed on acid-free paper that meets the
American National Standards Institute Z39.48 Standard.
Distributed in the United States by Random House, Inc.,
and in Canada by Random House of Canada Ltd

Library of Congress Cataloging-in-Publication Data

Trungpa, Chogyam, 1939–
The heart of the Buddha / Chogyam Trungpa.—1st ed.
p.   cm.—(Dharma ocean series : 1)
ISBN 0-87773-908-0
ISBN 0-87773-592-1 (pbk.)
1. Spiritual life (Buddhism)   2. Buddhism—China—
Tibet—Doctrines.   I. Title.   II. Series.
BQ7775.178   1991   90-52802
294.3′4448—dc20   CIP

Contents

Acknowledgments

I would like to thank the many people who worked on the development of the articles included in this book. Especially I would like to thank my fellow members of the Vajradhatu Editorial Office, who over the years have taken primary responsibility for the editing and production of Trungpa Rinpoche's written work, including: Sherab Chödzin, Carolyn Rose Gimian, and Sarah Coleman. Each of these editors trained directly with Trungpa Rinpoche in how best to convey his spoken teachings in written form, and in the appropriate forms and levels of editing for different occasions and audiences. The articles collected in *The Heart of the Buddha* exhibit the resulting variety of editorial styles. Sherab Chödzin, who was the first Vajradhatu editor-in-chief, was the original editor for several of the articles included in this collection. He also edited *Garuda Magazine,* where many of these articles were first published. Carolyn Gimian worked closely with Trungpa Rinpoche as my successor to the Vajradhatu editorial post and did the original editorial work on the "Sacred Outlook" article. She also did a careful reading of the book and gave much advice on the manuscript in its entirety. Sarah Coleman worked with Vajradhatu Editorial Office for many years, during which time she worked on a number of the articles in this collection.

The original production of the articles included in this collection involved the work of countless volunteers who carried out such tasks as tape recording, transcribing, typing, and manuscript checking. I would like to thank all of them for their donations of time and effort.

I would like to thank Mrs. Diana Mukpo for her kind permission to work with this material.

Most especially, I would like to thank the Venerable Chögyam Trungpa for his tireless efforts in leading students on the path of awakening.

Judith L. Lief
Editor

Editor's Foreword

The Heart of the Buddha is a collection of fifteen previously published articles by the Venerable Chögyam Trungpa, Rinpoche. In choosing the particular articles to be included, the intent was to introduce the reader to as complete a range of Rinpoche's teachings as possible. For that reason, both introductory essays and more technical or scholarly presentations have been included. Some articles were written for particular publications or for distribution among his students. Others were derived from seminars and talks he gave over his teaching career; as such, they embody the living quality of oral transmission and the importance of discussion and dialogue between student and teacher.

In his many seminars, Trungpa Rinpoche was careful always to balance the role of practice and of study. Students attending such seminars always spent time in formal meditation practice as well as in studying the Buddha's teachings through lectures, reading, and discussion groups. In that way, they could test their understanding through the mechanism of their own experience, so that refinement of intellectual understanding could be accompanied by a deepening of insight.

Personal Journey

At the heart of the Buddhist path is the practice of meditation. The development of mindfulness and awareness is an essential foundation for both understanding ourselves and working with others. It is a common preconception that the spiritual journey takes us away from ourselves, to some higher or more peaceful existence. In this context, meditation practice is seen as a kind of drug, or as a way of removing ourselves from the harsh realities of life. However, throughout his teachings, Trungpa Rinpoche stressed that meditation practice is not an escape but a way to "begin at the beginning."

In beginning the path, we need to be willing to confront ourselves directly, without either wishful thinking or harsh judgmentalism. Through the practice of meditation, we are constantly brought back to working with what is, rather than with what might be; we are constantly brought back to "square one." So at the heart of the very personal journey of meditation practice is the willingness simply to be who we are. It is a process of acceptance rather than one of manipulation.

While each student's journey is a solitary one, it is through the meeting of student and teacher that the spiritual path is awakened. The teacher-student relationship is of central importance in the Buddhist tradition. Devotion is the key to unlocking the power of the tradition. However, this concept is quite subtle, and we must be careful to distinguish genuine devotion from the naive approach of blind faith.

Stages on the Path

According to the Tibetan system, an individual student's journey has three main stages: *hinayana, mahayana,* and *vajrayana.* (In this context, these terms are simply descriptive of stages of the path and should not be confused with their more common usage as names for historical schools of Buddhist thought.) These three stages work together in a very powerful way. The hinayana marks the beginning stage, in which one explores the workings of one's own mind and emotions and begins to settle the mind through the practice of meditation. This allows one to lessen one's sense of struggle and to begin to make friends with oneself. In the second stage, mahayana, this friendliness begins to extend outward. There is a great appreciation for the phenomenal world as well as an understanding of the depth of suffering of fellow sentient beings. This gives rise to compassion and the intent to work for the benefit of others. The third stage, or vajrayana, is one of not holding back but of extending fearlessly to any situation that arises. There is a willingness to relate directly to the wisdom and power of one's mind and emotions, as evoked in visualization practice and tantric ritual.

While these may be viewed as three stages, they must all work together in a balanced way if the journey is to be successful. That is, each stage expands upon and enriches the previous stage, reawakening its insight in a broader context. So each serves to complement and enrich the others.

Working with Others

The insights gained through the formal practice of meditation can be applied to the variety of circumstances we encounter in our day-to-day lives. So daily life is not rejected, or viewed as simply a distraction to our "spiritual" practice.

Instead, by joining practice and ordinary life, the entirety of our experience is seen as valuable and, in fact, sacred.

Although classically trained in the ancient tradition of Tibetan Buddhism, Trungpa Rinpoche was immensely interested in the workings of modern society and in the social implications of the Buddhist teachings. Therefore he gave considerable attention in his talks and seminars to such issues as education, health care, the raising of children, the nature of relationships, and the conduct of business.

It is hoped that this collection of essays will give the reader a sense of the richness and variety of Trungpa Rinpoche's teachings and of their relevance in day-to-day life.

PART ONE

Personal Journey

What Is the Heart of the Buddha?

"Fundamentally speaking, ladies and gentlemen, here is the really good news, if we may call it that: We are intrinsically buddha and we are intrinsically good. Without exception and without the need for analytical studies, we can say that we automatically have buddha within us. That is known as buddha nature, or bodhichitta, the heart of the buddha."

In Buddhism, there are three codes of discipline, known as *shila*, *samadhi*, and *prajna*. *Shila* is discipline or conduct, a certain meditative way of behaving. *Samadhi* is the practice of mindfulness/awareness: the totality of your state of mind can be experienced without distraction. And *prajna*, or discriminating awareness, is the state of clarity in which you are able to distinguish different states of mind; you are no longer excited or depressed by particular states of mind. These three disciplines bring us to the next stage—of finally transcending the deception of ego, which is the experience of egolessness.

Egohood is the state of mind in which you are either repelled by or attracted to the phenomenal world. What you would like to see depends on your mentality, on what you think is desirable in order to maintain your "I am-ness," your

Based on a talk from "Conquering Ego's Deception," Cape Breton, 1981.

"me-ness." We are talking about transcending "I am-ness," "me-ness," which is called egolessness.

Egolessness doesn't mean that you are going to be completely dissolved into nothingness. In Western literature, Buddhism is often accused of saying this, especially in early Victorian Christian literature, as well as in various high school courses on Buddhism. They say Buddhists believe in nothingness, which is certainly not the case.

Egolessness means less "maniac-ness," in some sense—free from being an egomaniac. Egomania has several levels of subtlety. Ordinarily people think of an egomaniac as an obvious maniac, but if we study enough and look enough, we will see that there are subtleties of egomania. The dictators of the world could be seen as egomaniacal people, obviously, because they perform their functions in that way. But more ordinary people also function in that way, including ourselves in some sense. We would like to possess our world, and so we act in such a way that whatever we see around us is completely in order, according to our desire to maintain the security of "me," "myself"—which is egohood.

Inspired by means of shila, samadhi, and prajna—discipline, mediation, and discriminating awareness—we have freedom from egomaniac-ness, freedom from egohood. Beyond that, seeing through our own egomaniac-ness, we give birth to, or awaken, our innate greater existence, which is known as *bodhichitta* in Sanskrit.

Bodhi, which is related to *buddha*, literally means "awake." *Buddha* is a noun; *bodhi* is an epithet or an adjective for awakened ones, or for those who are in the process of awakening. *Chitta* is a Sanskrit word meaning "heart" or, occasionally, "essence." So *bodhichitta* is the essence of the buddha, the essence of the awakened ones.

We cannot give birth to the essence of the awakened ones unless we train, to begin with, in meditation practice: the *shamatha* discipline of mindfulness and the *vipashyana* discipline of awareness. Beyond that, it is necessary to fulfill the three disciplines of shila, samadhi, and prajna. That is, we know what to do and what not to do.

When we practice shila, samadhi, and prajna, we begin to be aware of the buddha in us. It is not that those principles *produce* buddhalike awareness particularly; we have that essence in us already. But shila, samadhi, and prajna bring us into the actual realization of who we are, what we are, finally.

According to the Buddhist tradition, we don't get *new* wisdom, nor does any foreign element come into our state of mind at all. Rather, it is a question of waking up and shedding our covers. We have those goodies in us already; we only have to uncover them.

The logic here is, if we have to transplant foreign goodieness into our system, it does not belong to us; it remains foreign. Because it is not part of us, it is likely to cease to exist at some point. Sooner or later, our basic nature is bound to reject that foreign transplant in our system. (Maybe this logic doesn't apply to heart transplants. These days they say if you have a foreign heart transplanted in you, you might live; you might survive.)

But here we are talking about awakening what we haven't already awakened. It is as if we have been kept in captivity and haven't been able to exercise our faculties properly; our activities have been controlled by circumstances. Giving birth to bodhichitta in one's heart, buddha in one's heart, brings extra freedom. That is the notion of *freedom* in Buddhism, altogether. Of course, when we talk about freedom, we are not talking about overthrowing the head of the state or anything like that: we are talking about freedom from the constriction of our own capabilities.

It is as if we were extraordinary children, possessing all sorts of genius, and we were being undermined by the society around us, which was dying to make us normal people. Whenever we would show any mark of genius, our parents would get embarrassed. They would try to put the lid on our pot, saying, "Charles, don't say those things. Just be like an ordinary person." That is what actually happens to us, with or without our parents.

I don't particularly want to blame our parents alone; we have also been doing this to ourselves. When we see something extraordinary, we are afraid to say so; we are afraid to express ourselves or to relate to such situations. So we put lids on ourselves—on our potential, our capabilities. But in Buddhism we are liberated from that kind of conventionality.

According to Buddhist terminology, *conventionality* refers to belief in habitual patterns. Conventional realities are synonymous with habitual patterns; and the authors of habitual patterns are ignorance and desire. Ignorance and desire go against shila discipline; they go against samadhi mindfulness, because they prevent us from keeping our minds on the point; and they go against prajna, because they develop dullness rather than discriminating sharpness.

Fundamentally speaking, ladies and gentlemen, here is the really good news, if we may call it that: We are intrinsically buddha and we are intrinsically good. Without exception, and without the need for analytical studies, we can say that we automatically have buddha within us. That is known as *buddha-nature*, or *bodhichitta*, the heart of the buddha.

We might ask ourselves, "What is the heart of the Buddha like? Does it think the way we do? Does it want to have fish and chips or is it just a pious heart that does nothing but religious things alone? Would that heart be the most holy heart of all, from a Christian point of view?" The answer is no. That heart is not necessarily pious.

The heart of the buddha is a very open heart. That heart would like to explore the phenomenal world; it is open to relating with others. That heart contains tremendous strength and confidence in itself, which is called fearlessness. That heart is also extremely inquisitive, which at this point is synonymous with prajna. It is expansive and sees in all directions. And that heart contains certain basic qualities, which we could call our true *basic genes*—our buddha-genes. We all possess those particular buddha-genes. Isn't it strange to say that the mind has genes? But it turns out to be true.

These buddha-genes have two characteristics. First, they are able to see through, as well as not be afraid of, the reality of the phenomenal world. We might come up with obstacles and difficulties of all kinds, but those particular genes are not afraid to deal with them. We just shed the coverings of such possibilities as we go along. Second, these genes also contain gentleness; they are ever so loving, which goes beyond just being kind. They are extremely tender and capable of reflecting themselves, even to those who don't want to relate with them. And they are absolutely free from any form of aggression. They are so soft and kind.

The buddha-genes are also full of a sense of humor and delight, which is referred to as *great joy*. When you are able to experience that such genes exist within you, you begin to feel cheerful and smile and have a sense of humor.

There are two different kinds of humor. One kind of humor comes from not taking the world seriously: you come up with all sorts of jokes about other people's problems. The other kind is a general sense of joy. Nothing is regarded as downgrading; everything is uplifted, constantly. Here we are talking about the second kind of humor.

From the practitioner's point of view, we have all sorts of disciplines to awaken our enlightened genes. The main discipline is known as exchanging oneself for other. That is to say, we completely identify with others' pain; and we project out, or give away, pleasure altogether. In that way, we begin to see through, and actually expose, the clumsiness of how we hold onto ourselves.

Let us have a short discussion.

STUDENT: Rinpoche, I was wondering about the second characteristic of the buddha-genes. Is this tender loving quality present all the time or just at certain moments?

TRUNGPA RINPOCHE: That's an interesting question. Can I ask you a question back? Does a fire have the potential of blazing when it's at the level of a spark? What would you say?

S: I guess it depends on the circumstances.

TR: What kind of circumstances would they be?

S: Well, if you were in a garage with gas fumes, or if you were out in an open field—

TR: Sure, sure. But, intrinsically speaking, in itself does it have that potential?

S: I will agree that it could blaze up.

TR: It could blaze up and blow up our garage, right? I am talking about exactly the same thing. In itself, the buddha-gene is capable of the whole thing.

STUDENT: Sir, what is the difference between meditation-in-action and sitting meditation? I have the impression that when I am working on a sculpture in my studio, lots of insight is given to me. That seems as important to me as straight sitting. Is there anything wrong with that?

TRUNGPA RINPOCHE: Well, it's an interesting point, you see. We were just talking about fire. Somebody first has to make the fire; then it blazes. In the same way, you might have the intuition that you don't have to do sitting practice. You might feel you have the experience of that already, which I don't doubt. Probably a lot of people do. Nonetheless, we do need some kind of field training. We have to know how to relate with reality, and we also have to know how to develop discipline. If we sit and practice shamatha-vipashyana meditation, probably nothing will happen for a long period of time. And the idea isn't that anything *should* happen to us. We are just silent.

At the end of the letter you sent me, you signed off *paix*, "peace." Real peace is nonaction; that is the source of all action. We have to learn how to be a rock in order to be a tree or a flower or wind or lightning or a typhoon. We have to be still, then we go beyond that. Therefore sitting practice is very important.

We are not particularly training ourselves to destroy or conquer the world. We are trying to relate to the world in the same way that we relate to the birth of our first child or, for that matter, to our own orgasm—which happens, I hope, when we make love. Anything active that happens has some relationship to that very stillness. That stillness is not vacant or deadly; it is full of energy, automatically.

So that is the difference between postmeditation and meditation itself. Meditation prepares us for action, and sometimes action prepares us for nonaction. It is like breathing in and out: when you breathe out, it's action; but in order to breathe out you have to breathe in again. It goes on that way. So it is important to have a very strict discipline of being still and solid. Out of that comes a lot of energy and a lot of wisdom. Meditation and postmeditation are equally valid in our lives—just as breathing in and breathing out are both important.

S: *Merci beaucoup*.

STUDENT: Rinpoche, could you say a little bit about vipashyana mediation? You mentioned it in your talk, but I'm not really sure what it is.

TRUNGPA RINPOCHE: *Vipashyana* is a Sanskrit word which

literally means "seeing clearly." In Tibetan we use the word *lhakthong*. *Lhak* means "superior" and *thong* means "seeing." So *lhakthong* means "clear seeing," "superior seeing."

Vipashyana begins once we have developed substantial shamatha discipline of being precise and mindful, on the spot, all the time. In shamatha, sound, smell, feeling, thought process, and everything else are looked at, but with such precision that they are nothing other than stillness. They don't produce further bubbles, or further percolation, of any kind at all.

You might say, "Ah, I thought of my father telling me no." At that moment, both your father and the idea of him saying "No, don't do that" are divided into now, now, now, all the time. Everything is chopped into that level of precision, into a grain of sand. That is shamatha.

Usually, memory is predominant in everything you experience. If you are sitting in a meditation hall and the smell of food comes from the kitchen, you think about what kind of dinner they are cooking for you. Or else, you feel the ache in your buttocks and back and you want to shift around. Shamatha means that everything is simply looked at. It is sliced up, but not aggressively; it is just looked at—look, look, look.

Through shamatha you are capable of looking at these experiences as individual entities, without referring to the past and without thinking about where they are going, or what they are going to do to you. Everything is without beginning and without end, just on the spot. If you think of onion soup and how you would like to go out and *get* onion soup, it is only on the level of thought. So you chop your thoughts—now, now, now.

Out of that comes vipashyana. On the level of vipashyana, you chop thoughts because of your training in shamatha, but at the same time you bring them along. The world is a panoramic view, but at the same time things really don't hang together the way they ordinarily used to.

Things are made out of pieces of simple realities, primitive realities. Even if you smell onions for a long time—for half an hour—those smells are chopped into pieces: you smell them, then you don't smell them, you smell them, then you don't smell them. Otherwise, if there were no gap, you couldn't smell at all.

Experiences are not continuous at the ego level. We think they are all together, in cahoots, but it doesn't really happen that way. Everything is made out of dots. When experiences are chopped into small pieces, some realization of the unity of the display could come out of that. That is vipashyana.

You begin to feel good when, for instance, you touch a rock, because you feel that the rock is not a continuous rock, but the rock of the moment. When you hold your fan, it is the fan of the moment; when you blink, your blink is of the moment; when you meet your friends, they are friends of the moment. Nothing is expected and nothing is demanded any more. Everything is seen clearly.

Clear seeing: that is the definition of vipashyana, which is the result of shamatha. Things could be seen as a great display, as a Disney world, or whatever you want to call it. You realize that things are not all that together. But because they are not together, they are fantastically colorful. The more you see the mark of discontinuity, the more you see things as colorful. In order to see color you have to take a rest; then you see color again. So you see, you rest, and then you see brilliance again. That is the precision of how to perceive the phenomenal world.

STUDENT: Rinpoche, you said to an earlier questioner that you hoped he would have pleasure experiencing his orgasm. In my experience, I have some confusion about whether pleasure is pleasurable. Since I haven't gotten over aggression and passion, how can I relate to things at all—if pleasure isn't pleasurable and pain isn't particularly painful, and I'm still caught in that way?

TRUNGPA RINPOCHE: Well, the point is that there is no such thing as pleasure per se. In other words, different people experience so-called pleasure entirely differently, depending on their state of mind, where they are coming from, and how they are going to proceed after the pleasure. Pleasure is not a solid thing.

Sometimes people get very angry and discouraged when they go back to a restaurant where they had great pleasure before, and they find that the food is lousy and the service is not so good. So they complain to the manager.

One doesn't get the expected services or expected situations *any* time. I am not the same Trungpa you saw a few days ago. I am a fresh, new Trungpa—right now! And I will always be that way. I will be dead and gone tonight, and right now, this very moment, I am dying and being born. So the next time I give a talk, I will be entirely different.

You can't rely on one particular reference point. In some sense that is extraordinarily fresh and feels good, but on the other hand it may be sad, because you want to hang onto the past, constantly. Until there's enough familiarity with the mentality of shamatha and vipashyana, you won't understand this. And that practice of shamatha/vipashyana goes on, up to the level of vajrayana discipline, as well.

When you see a fantastic display, it is chopped into little pieces. This allows you to breathe, because there's a gap between the pieces; therefore you begin to appreciate those pieces altogether. I don't think I can say it more vividly than that. You actually have to do it. "Seeing is believing," as they say in the English language.

S: Thank you very much.

TR: You're more than welcome.

STUDENT: Sir, earlier tonight you were talking about how we put a lid on ourselves, and how it is the nature of one's heart to be inquisitive. And yet within Buddhism there is a notion of ethics. There are certain ways to do things and certain ways not to do things.

In my own personal experience, when I feel inquisitive sometimes I flash back on Buddhist ethics, as a reference point for whether I am doing the proper thing. But I sometimes wonder how much I should stick to the scriptures and how much I should just go ahead and be inquisitive. My question is, how does one know when to put a lid on oneself and when to go forward?

TRUNGPA RINPOCHE: It's purely up to you. That is to say, you have to have enough training, or at least understanding of the momentariness of your mind. Your mind doesn't continue, therefore you appreciate the world. Then you can go on to explore further.

There is no particular dogma that goes with that; there's no particular guideline either, apart from having erect posture and imitating the Buddha. You can do that. You will never be referred to as being presumptuous.

S: So, I should just keep on practicing.

TR: Keep on practicing, yes.

2

Intellect and Intuition

"*The transition from knowledge to wisdom is not simply one of first acquiring knowledge and then suddenly becoming wise. The definition of wisdom is that one intuitively knows everything already; it is independent of amassing information. But we do not seem to know how to make this transition from intellect to wisdom. There seems to be a very big gap between them, and we are uncertain as to how to handle it, how to become both a scholar and a yogi. We seem to need a mediator. That mediator is compassion, or warmth: knowledge is transformed into wisdom by means of compassion.*"

There seem to be two distinct approaches to the spiritual path: the intellectual and the intuitive. In the intellectual tradition, spiritual development is viewed as a sharpening of intellectual precision, primarily through the study of theology. Whereas in the intuitive or mystical tradition, spiritual development is viewed as a deepening of awareness or devotion through practices such as meditation. However, neither the intellectual nor the intuitive approach is complete without the other. These two approaches are not in opposition to one another. Rather they are two channels which combine to form the spiritual path.

Opening talk, 1973 Vajradhatu Seminary, Teton Village, Wyoming.

Let us examine the intellectual and intuitive traditions in more detail. In the West, the intellectual tradition has for a long time been predominant. And in some Buddhist countries the emphasis on scholasticism has grown so strong that Buddhist scholars have completely lost touch with the meditative tradition. Buddhists who emphasize the scholarly side of the teaching frequently feel that it is dangerous to begin meditating until they have mastered the theory. So they begin the spiritual path by studying very intensely and becoming extremely learned. But then, when they have discovered everything intellectually and completely mastered the theories of Buddhism, they feel they no longer need to meditate because they have all the answers already. Adherents of this approach view the Buddha as a superscholar and enlightenment as being totally informed.

Adherents of the intuitive tradition, on the other hand, regard study and analysis as obstacles to spiritual development. Seeing the irrelevance of acquiring knowledge disconnected from personal experience, they tend to react by rejecting the intellectual approach altogether. Instead they stress the practice of meditation as the only way to develop insight. From their viewpoint, in order to attain enlightenment one does not need to know anything at all. The Buddha is regarded as the perfect meditator, and the more beautifully one can sit and meditate, the closer one is to enlightenment.

By focusing on only one aspect of experience, each of these approaches to spirituality remains only partial. The contemplative traditions of Buddhism, such as the Tibetan and Zen traditions, while emphasizing meditation practice very strongly, see study as something which should go alongside it. It is felt that a student cannot rely on meditation practice alone without sharpening his intelligence. The idea is that one first needs some grounding in meditation practice. Then one can begin to work with the intellectual aspect of the tradition. In this way study becomes a confirmation of experience rather than simply the acquisition of banks of irrelevant information. Rather than becoming a stupid meditator or an absent-minded intellectual, the student can become an intelligent yogi—a scholar and a practitioner at the same time.

The notion of enlightenment transcends the limitations of both the contemplative and the scholarly traditions. As a description of human wholeness, it expresses the flavor of the Buddhist approach to spirituality. The dawn of enlightenment could be described as a form of absorption. But that does not mean it is a trancelike state in which one loses contact with the world around one. It is a sense of totality and a sense of openness which does not seem to have any beginning or end. Such a state of being is known as *vajralike samadhi*. The notion of *vajra* is that of psychological indestructibility. Because that quality of sanity does not have any gaps of faults, because it is thoroughly united with its own faculties, it cannot be destroyed. And *samadhi* refers to the stillness of intelligence, which is self-existing rather than constantly speeding along trying to find a conclusion to everything. Vajralike samadhi is a threefold process consisting of *prajna,* which is the highest form of intellect; *karuna,* which is the highest form of compassion; and *jnana,* which is the highest form of wisdom.

Prajna, or intellect, is completely intuitive as well as intellectually precise. The working of prajna is such that when we pay proper attention to persons or situations they automatically give us answers or understanding. So we do not have to analyze or to cultivate our intelligence anymore. That quality of intelligence seems to be all-pervasive—but at the same time it is to the point. It is sharp, precise, and direct, but not in the limited manner of a chisel or a thumbtack.

Karuna, or compassion, is another attribute of the process of samadhi. *Karuna* is usually translated as "compassion." However, the word *compassion* is filled with connotations in English which have nothing to do with karuna. So it is important to clarify what is meant by enlightened compassion and how it differs from our usual notion of compassion. Usually we think of a compassionate person as someone who is kind and gentle and who never loses his temper. Such a person is always willing to forgive our mistakes and to comfort us. But enlightened compassion is not quite as simpleminded as that notion of a kindly, well-meaning soul.

An analogy often used in the Buddhist tradition is that true compassion is like a fish and prajna is like water. That is, intellect and compassion are dependent on one another, but at the same time, each has its own life and its own functions. Compassion is a state of calmness; it also involves intelligence and enormous vitality. Without intelligence and skillfulness, compassion can degenerate into a bungling sort of charity. For instance, if we give food to someone who is extremely hungry, he will temporarily recover from his hunger. But he gets hungry every day. And if we keep giving food to that person, eventually he will learn that whenever he is hungry he can get food from us. At that point we have succeeded in turning that person into a jellyfish who is unwilling to explore the possibility of getting food for himself. Such an approach is, in fact, uncompassionate compassion, or compassion without skillful means. It is known as *idiot compassion*.

True compassion is spacious and wise as well as resourceful. In this type of compassion we do not just blindly launch into a project but we look into situations dispassionately. There is a sense of priorities as to which situations should be handled immediately and which are worth putting off. This type of compassion could be called *intelligent love* or *intelligent affection*. We know how to express our affection so that it does not destroy a person but instead helps him to develop. It is more like a dance than a hug. And the music behind it is that of prajna, or intellect.

So the stage is set by the dance of compassion and the music of prajna. And the setting in which this dance takes place is known as jnana, or wisdom, which is the whole perspective, the entire panorama.

Let us examine in greater detail how these three qualities of enlightenment—knowledge, compassion, and wisdom—are interrelated. We begin with prajna, or knowledge: we need to know where we are; we have to explore our environment, our particular location in time and space. So knowledge comes first, and wisdom comes later. Once we have knowledge as to where we are, then we can become wise because we do not have to struggle with our bearings. We do not have to fight for our position. So, in a sense, wisdom is an expression of nonviolence: we do not have to fight for it because we are already wise.

The transition from knowledge to wisdom is not simply one of first acquiring knowledge and then suddenly becoming wise. The definition of *wisdom* is that one intuitively knows everything already; it is independent of amassing information. But we do not seem to know how to make this transition from intellect to wisdom. There seems to be a very big gap between them, and we are uncertain as to how to handle it, how to become both a scholar and a yogi. We seem to need a mediator. That mediator is compassion, or warmth: knowledge is transformed into wisdom by means of compassion.

We may begin by collecting all kinds of information, trying to become great scholars or walking books. In fact, prajna is a very scholarly process in which we acquire enormous amounts of information and logic. At this level we can handle our experience logically, even mathematically. But how do we make that knowledge part of ourselves rather than purely an assortment of lists of information?

When we develop prajna in its fullest sense, psychologically and spiritually, then we may begin to develop a sense of friendliness or warmth not only toward ourselves but also toward the world. This does not mean boosting our egos—patting ourselves on the back for all the Ph.D.'s we have earned. Instead friendliness is a kind of fascination for our collection of ideas and knowledge; we have become fascinated by the world and extremely curious as to what it is all about. For instance, in the West great scientists like Einstein have been known to become rather eccentric. They seem to transcend ordinary logic and to become extremely individualistic. As they become absorbed by their knowledge, or prajna, they begin to develop a quality of softness or eccentricity. That eccentricity seems to be the area of compassion, in which there is room to journey back and forth between being wise and being knowledgeable. In this state of mind, there is no gap between intellect and intuition. Instead, there is simply a further development of energy, which is called compassion.

As the energy of compassion develops, we begin to celebrate what we have discovered. We begin to like the knowledge we have acquired. We have seen the way things work, and now we begin to take that understanding personally. We would like to share it with everyone. There is an enormous celebration taking place. We do not need to prove our ideas to anybody, and we do not feel that we are under attack. There is a sense of joy in being part of this knowledge, and that sense of joy, which triggers the transition from knowledge to wisdom, is compassion, or unconditional love.

It seems to take a long time for us to get to the point of being wise, where we no longer need external reinforcement or encouragement—or, in fact, any external reference point at all. Such wisdom is extremely inventive; rather than needing to study each detail of a particular area, we simply sense the whole area intuitively and very precisely. We are very much in tune with things. That is why the Buddha is known as the Omniscient One. It is not because he was a great scholar who read all the books and therefore had all the information, but because he had an accurate general sense of everything. At the level of wisdom, or jnana, all the conceptual master plans of the world or the universe have been seen through, so facts and figures do not play a particularly important part.

As individuals on the spiritual path, we experience more and more glimpses of this enlightened state. To give a somewhat negative analogy, if we develop a terminal illness, at first we may feel an attack of sickness just once a month. But as we go on, our sickness becomes worse and the attacks become more frequent, maybe once a day. Then the attacks of sickness come every day—in fact, several times a day. And finally we face death because the attacks of sickness are constant; the sickness has become overwhelming. The death of ego, or the development of enlightenment, happens in the same way. We do not consciously have to create the experience of enlightenment—it just happens. It comes to us as our life situations evolves.

3

The Four Foundations of Mindfulness

"As far as meditation practice is concerned, in meditation we work on this thing, rather than on trying to sort out the problem from the outside. We work on the projector rather than the projection. We turn inward, instead of trying to sort out external problems of A, B, and C. We work on the creator of duality rather than the creation. That is beginning at the beginning."

For the follower of the *buddhadharma*, the teachings of Buddhism, there is a need for great emphasis on the practice of meditation. One must see the straightforward logic that mind is the cause of confusion and that by transcending confusion one attains the enlightened state. This can only take place through the practice of meditation. The Buddha himself experienced this, by working on his own mind; and what he learned has been handed down to us.

Mindfulness is a basic approach to the spiritual journey that is common to all traditions of Buddhism. But before we begin to look closely at that approach, we should have some idea of what is meant by spirituality itself. Some say that

Remarks on meditation practice, 1973 Vajradhatu Seminary.

spirituality is a way of attaining a better kind of happiness, transcendental happiness. Others see it as a benevolent way to develop power over others. Still others say the point of spirituality is to acquire magical powers so we can change our bad world into a good world or purify the world through miracles. It seems that all of these points of view are irrelevant to the Buddhist approach. According to the buddhadharma, spirituality means relating with the working basis of one's existence, which is one's state of mind.

There is a problem with one's basic life, one's basic being. This problem is that we are involved in a continual struggle to survive, to maintain our position. We are continually trying to grasp onto some solid image of ourselves. And then we have to defend that particular fixed conception. So there is warfare, there is confusion, and there is passion and aggression; there are all kinds of conflicts. From the Buddhist point of view, the development of true spirituality is cutting through our basic fixation, that clinging, that stronghold of something-or-other, which is known as ego.

In order to do that we have to find out what ego is. What is this all about? Who are we? We have to look into our already existing state of mind. And we have to understand what practical step we can take to do that. We are not involved here in a metaphysical discussion about the purpose of life and the meaning of spirituality on an abstract level. We are looking at this question from the point of view of a working situation. We need to find some simple thing we can do in order to embark on the spiritual path.

People have difficulty beginning a spiritual practice because they put a lot of energy into looking for the best and easiest way to get into it. We might have to change our attitude and give up looking for the best or the easiest way. Actually, there is no choice. Whatever approach we take, we will have to deal with what we are already. We have to look at who we are. According to the Buddhist tradition, the working basis of the path and the energy involved in the path is the mind—one's own mind, which is working in us all the time.

Spirituality is based on mind. In Buddhism, mind is what distinguishes sentient beings from rocks or trees or bodies of water. That which possesses discriminating awareness, that which possesses a sense of duality—which grasps or rejects something external—that is mind. Fundamentally, it is that which can associate with an "other"—with any "something" that is perceived as different from the perceiver. That is the definition of mind. The traditional Tibetan phrase defining mind means precisely that: "That which can think of the other, the projection, is mind."

So by mind we mean something very specific. It is not just something very vague and creepy inside our heads or hearts, something that just happens as part of the way the wind blows and the grass grows. Rather, it is something very concrete. It contains perception—perception that is very uncomplicated, very basic, very precise. Mind develops its particular nature as that perception begins to linger on something other than oneself. Mind makes the fact of perceiving something else stand for the existence of oneself. That is the mental trick that constitutes mind. In fact, it should be the opposite. Since the perception starts from oneself, the logic should be: "I exist, therefore the other exists." But somehow the hypocrisy of mind is developed to such an extent that mind lingers on the other as a way of getting the feedback that it itself exists, which is a fundamentally erroneous belief. It is the fact that the existence of self is questionable that motivates the trick of duality.

This mind is our working basis for the practice of meditation and the development of awareness. But mind is something more than the process of confirming self by the dualistic lingering on the other. Mind also includes what are known as *emotions,* which are the highlights of mental states. Mind cannot exist without emotions. Daydreaming and discursive thoughts are not enough. Those alone would be too boring. The dualistic trick would wear too thin. So we tend to create waves of emotion which go up and down: passion, aggression, ignorance, pride—all kinds of emotions. In the beginning we create them deliberately, as a game of trying to prove to ourselves that we exist. But eventually the game becomes a hassle; it becomes more than a game and forces us to challenge ourselves more than we intended. It is like a hunter who, for the sport of practicing his shooting, decides to shoot one leg of a deer at a time. But the deer runs very fast, and it appears it might get away altogether. This becomes a total challenge to the hunter, who rushes after the deer, now trying to kill it completely, to shoot it in the heart. So the hunter has been challenged and feels defeated by his own game.

Emotions are like that. They are not a requirement for survival; they are a game we developed that went wrong at some point—it went sour. In the face of this predicament we feel terribly frustrated and absolutely helpless. Such frustration causes some people to fortify their relationship to the "other" by creating a god or other projections, such as saviors, gurus, and mahatmas. We create all kinds of projections as henchmen, hitmen, to enable us to redominate our territory. The implicit sense is that if we pay homage to such great beings, they will function as our helpers, as the guarantors of our ground.

So we have created a world that is bittersweet. Things are amusing but, at the same time, not so amusing. Sometimes things seem terribly funny but, on the other hand, terribly sad. Life has the quality of a game of ours that has trapped us. The setup of mind has created the whole thing. We might complain about the government or the economy of the country or the prime rate of interest, but those factors are secondary. The original process at the root of the problems is the competitiveness of seeing oneself only as a reflection of the other. Problematic situations arise automatically as expressions of that. They are our own production, our own neat work. And that is what is called mind.

According to the Buddhist tradition, there are eight types of consciousness and fifty-two types of conceptions and all kinds of other aspects of mind, about which we do not have to go into detail. All these aspects are based largely on the primeval dualistic approach. There are the spiritual aspects and the psychological aspects and all sorts of other aspects. All are bound up in the realm of duality, which is ego.

As far as meditation practice is concerned, in meditation we work on *this* thing, rather than on trying to sort out the problem from the outside. We work on the projector rather than the projection. We turn inward, instead of trying to sort out external problems of *A, B,* and *C.* We work on the creator of duality rather than the creation. That is beginning at the beginning.

According to the Buddhist tradition, there are three main aspects of mind, which in Tibetan are called *sem, rikpa,* and *yi.* The basic mind, the simple capacity for duality we have already described, is *sem. Rikpa* literally means "intelligence" or "brightness." In colloquial Tibetan, if you say that somebody has rikpa, it means he is a clever, sharp fellow. This sharpness of rikpa is a kind of side function that develops from the basic mind; it is a kind of lawyer's mentality that everybody develops. Rikpa looks at a problem from various angles and analyzes the possibilities of different ways of approaching it. It looks at a problem in every possible way—inside-out and outside-in.

The third aspect, *yi,* is traditionally classified as the sixth sense consciousness. The first five sense consciousnesses are sight, smell, taste, hearing, and touch, and the sixth is yi. Yi is mental sensitivity. It is associated with the heart and is a kind of balancing factor that acts as a switchboard in relation to the other five sense consciousnesses. When you see a sight and hear a sound at the same time, the sight and sound are synchronized by the sixth sense to constitute aspects of a single event. Yi does a kind of automatic synchronization, or automatic computerization, of the whole process of sense experience. You can see, smell, hear, taste, and feel all at the same time, and all of those inputs are coherently workable. They make sense to you because of yi.

So yi is a sort of central-headquarters switchboard which coordinates experience into a coherent whole. In some sense it is the most important of all the three aspects of mind. It is not as intelligent in the sense of manipulation as sem. Sem has something of a political attitude toward one's relationship with the world; it is somewhat strategy oriented. The sixth sense is more domestic in function. It just tries to maintain the coordination of experience so that all information comes through efficiently and there is no problem of being out of communication with anything that is going on. On the other hand, rikpa, which is the intelligence—the research worker, as it were—in this administration of mind, takes an overall view of one's whole situation. It surveys the relationship between mind and the sixth sense and tries to search out all the possibilities of where things are going wrong, where things might go wrong, where things have gone wrong, how things could be put right. This research worker does not have the power actually to take action on the level of external relations. It is more like an advisor to the State Department.

These three principles of sem, rikpa, and yi are the most important for us to be aware of at this point. Many other aspects of mind are described in the traditional literature, but these three will suffice for our present understanding.

We should consider this understanding not so much as something that we have been told and therefore we should believe in. The experience described here can actually be felt personally. It can be worked on, related to. A certain part of our experience is organized by basic mind, a certain part by the sixth sense, and a certain part by intelligence. In order to understand the basic functions of mindfulness-awareness practice, I think it is very important for us to understand and realize these complexities of mind.

A gigantic world of mind exists to which we are almost totally unexposed. This whole world—this tent and this microphone, this light, this grass, the very pair of spectacles that we are wearing—is made by mind. Minds made this up, put these things together. Every bolt and nut was put in by somebody-or-other's mind. This whole world is mind's world, the product of mind. This is needless to say; I am sure everybody knows this. But we might remind ourselves of it so that we realize that meditation is not an exclusive activity that involves forgetting this world and getting into something else. By meditating, we are dealing with the very mind that devised our eyeglasses and put the lenses in the rims, and the very mind that put up this tent. Our coming here is the product of our minds. Each of us has different mental manifestations, which permit others to identify us and say, "This guy is named so-and-so, this girl is named so-and-so." We can be identified as individuals because we have different mental approaches, which also shape the expressions of our physical features. Our physical characteristics are part of our mental activity as well. So this is a living world, mind's world. Realizing this, working with mind is no longer a remote or mysterious thing to do. It is no longer dealing with something that is hidden or somewhere else.

Mind is right here. Mind is hanging out in the world. It is an open secret.

The method for beginning to relate directly with mind, which was taught by Lord Buddha and which has been in use for the past twenty-five hundred years, is the practice of mindfulness. There are four aspects to this practice, traditionally known as the Four Foundations of Mindfulness.

Mindfulness of Body

Mindfulness of body, the first foundation of mindfulness, is connected with the need for a sense of being, a sense of groundedness.

To begin with, there is some problem about what we understand by *body*. We sit on chairs or on the ground; we eat; we sleep; we wear clothes. But the body we relate with in going through these activities is questionable. According to the tradition, the body we think we have is what is known as psychosomatic body. It is largely based on projections and concepts of body. This psychosomatic body contrasts with the enlightened person's sense of body, which might be called *body-body*. This sense of body is free from conceptualizations. It is just simple and straightforward. There is a direct relationship with the earth. As for us, we do not actually have a relationship with the earth. We have some relationship with body, but it is very uncertain and erratic. We flicker back and forth between body and something else—fantasies, ideas. That seems to be our basic situation.

Even though the psychosomatic body is constituted by projections of body, it can be quite solid in terms of those projections. We have expectations concerning the existence of this body, therefore we have to refuel it, entertain it, wash it. Through this psychosomatic body we are able to experience a sense of being. For instance, as you listen to this talk, you feel that you are sitting on the ground. Your buttocks are resting on the earth; therefore you can extend your legs and lean back a little so you have less strain on your body. All of this affects your sense of being. You have some sense of relaxation as opposed to how it would be if you were standing—standing on your feet, standing on your toes, or standing on your palms. The posture that you are adopting at the moment seems to be an agreeable one; in fact it is one of the most congenial postures that one could ever think of. So being in this posture, you can relax and listen—you can listen to something other than the demands of your body.

Sitting down now, you feel somewhat settled. On the other hand, if the ground were very damp, you would not feel so settled. Then you would begin to perch on the ground, like a bird on a branch. This would be another matter altogether. If you are intensely concerned with some event about to happen or if you are worried about some encounter you are about to have—for example, if you are being interviewed for a job by some executive—you don't really sit on your chair, you perch on it. Perching happens when some demand is being made on you and you feel less of your body and more of your tension and nervousness. It involves a very different sense of body and of being than if you are just sitting, as you are doing now.

Right now you are sitting on the ground, and you are so completely sitting down that you have been able to shift gears and turn on your tape recorders, or even start taking notes, and you do not regard that as doing two things at once. You sit there, you have totally flopped, so to speak, and, having done that, you can turn to your other perceptions—listening, looking, and so on.

But your sitting here at this point is not actually very much a matter of your *body* per se sitting on the ground; it is far more a matter of your psychosomatic body sitting on the ground. Sitting on the ground as you are—all facing in one direction, toward the speaker; being underneath the roof of the tent; being attracted to the light that is focused on the stage—all gives you a particular idea; it creates a certain style of participation, which is the condition of your psychosomatic body. You are somewhat involved in sitting per se, but at the same time you are not. Mind is doing it; concept is doing it. Your mind is shaping the situation in accordance with your body. Your mind is sitting on the ground. Your mind is taking notes. Your mind is wearing glasses. Your mind has such-and-such a hairdo; your mind is wearing such-and-such clothes. Everyone is creating a world according to the body situation, but largely out of contact with it. That is the psychosomatic process.

Mindfulness of body brings this all-pervasive mind-imitating-body activity into the practice of meditation. The practice of meditation has to take into account that mind continually shapes itself into body*like* attitudes. Consequently, since the time of Buddha, sitting meditation has been recommended and practiced, and it has proved to be the best way of dealing with this situation. The basic technique that goes with sitting meditation is working with the breath. You identify with the breath, particularly with the outbreath. The inbreath is just a gap, a space. During the inbreath you just wait. So you breathe out and then you dissolve and then there is a gap. Breathe out . . . dissolve . . . gap. An openness, an expansion, can take place constantly that way.

Mindfulness plays a very important role in this technique. In this case, mindfulness means that when you sit and meditate, you actually do sit. You actually do sit as far as the psychosomatic body is concerned. You feel the ground, body, breath, temperature. You don't try specifically to watch and keep track of what is going on. You don't try to formalize the sitting situation and make it into some special activity that you are performing. You just sit. And then you begin to feel that there is some sense of groundedness. This is not particularly a product of being deliberate, but it is more the force of the actual fact of being there. So you sit. And you sit. And you breathe. And you sit and you breathe. Sometimes you think, but still you are thinking sitting thoughts. The psychosomatic body is sitting, so your thoughts have a flat bottom.

Mindfulness of body is connected with the earth. It is an openness that has a base, a foundation. A quality of expansive awareness develops through mindfulness of body—a sense of being settled and of therefore being able to afford to open out.

Going along with this mindfulness requires a great deal of trust. Probably the beginning meditator will not be able simply to rest there, but will feel the need for a change. I remember someone who had just finished a retreat telling me how she had sat and felt her body and felt grounded. But then she had thought immediately how she should be doing something else. And she went on to tell me how the right book had "just jumped" into her lap, and she had started to read. At that point one doesn't have a solid base anymore. One's mind is beginning to grow little wings. Mindfulness of body has to do with trying to remain human, rather than becoming an animal or fly or etheric being. It means just trying to remain a human being, an ordinary human being.

The basic starting point for this is solidness, groundedness. When you sit, you actually sit. Even your floating thoughts begin to sit on their own bottoms. There are no particular problems. You have a sense of solidness and groundedness, and, at the same time, a sense of being.

Without this particular foundation of mindfulness, the

rest of your meditation practice could be very airy-fairy—
vacillating back and forth, trying this and trying that. You
could be constantly tiptoeing on the surface of the universe,
not actually getting a foothold anywhere. You could become
an eternal hitchhiker. So with this first technique you develop some basic solidness. In mindfulness of body, there is
a sense of finding some home ground.

Mindfulness of Life

The application of mindfulness has to be precise. If we cling
to our practice, we create stagnation. Therefore, in our application of the techniques of mindfulness, we must be aware
of the fundamental tendency to cling, to survive. We come
to this in the second foundation of mindfulness, which is
mindfulness of life, or survival. Since we are dealing with
the context of meditation, we encounter this tendency in the
form of clinging to the meditative state. We experience the
meditative state and it is momentarily tangible, but in that
same moment it is also dissolving. Going along with this
process means developing a sense of letting go of awareness
as well as of contacting it. This basic technique of the
second foundation of mindfulness could be described as
touch-and-go: you are there—present, mindful—and then you
let go.

A common misunderstanding is that the meditative state
of mind has to be captured and then nursed and cherished.
That is definitely the wrong approach. If you try to domesti-
cate your mind through meditation—try to possess it by
holding onto the meditative state—the clear result will be
regression on the path, with a loss of freshness and spontaneity. If you try to hold on without lapse all the time, then
maintaining your awareness will begin to become a domestic
hassle. It will become like painfully going through house-

work. There will be an underlying sense of resentment, and the practice of meditation will become confusing. You will begin to develop a love-hate relationship toward your practice, in which your concept of it seems good, but, at the same time, the demand this rigid concept makes on you is too painful.

So the technique of the mindfulness of life is based on touch-and-go. You focus your attention on the object of awareness, but then, in the same moment, you disown that awareness and go on. What is needed here is some sense of confidence—confidence that you do not have to securely own your mind, but that you can tune into its process spontaneously.

Mindfulness of life relates to the clinging tendency not only in connection with the meditative state, but, even more importantly, in connection with the level of raw anxiety about survival that manifests in us constantly, second by second, minute by minute. You breathe for survival; you lead your life for survival. The feeling is constantly present that you are trying to protect yourself from death. For the practical purposes of the second foundation, instead of regarding this survival mentality as something negative, instead of relating to it as ego-clinging as is done in the abstract philosophical overview of Buddhism, this particular practice switches logic around. In the second foundation, the survival struggle is regarded as a steppingstone in the practice of meditation. Whenever you have the sense of the survival instinct functioning, that can be transmuted into a sense of being, a sense of having already survived. Mindfulness becomes a basic acknowledgment of existing. This does not have the flavor of "Thank God, I have survived." Instead, it is more objective, impartial: "I am alive, I am here, so be it."

We may undertake the practice of meditation with a sense

of purity or austerity. We somehow feel that by meditating we are doing the right thing, and we feel like good boys or good girls. Not only are we doing the right thing, but we are also getting away from the ugly world. We are becoming pure; we are renouncing the world and becoming like the yogis of the past. We don't actually live and meditate in a cave, but we can regard the corner of the room that we have arranged for meditation as a cave. We can close our eyes and feel that we are meditating in a cave in the mountains. That kind of imagination makes us feel rather good. It feels fitting; it feels clean and secure.

This strong tendency is an attempt to isolate the practice of meditation from one's actual living situation. We build up all kinds of extraneous concepts and images about it. It is satisfying to regard meditation as austere and above life. But mindfulness of life steers us in just the opposite direction. The approach of mindfulness of life is that if you are meditating in a room, you are meditating in a room. You don't regard the room as a cave. If you are breathing, you are breathing, rather than convincing yourself you are a motionless rock. You keep your eyes open and simply let yourself be where you are. There are no imaginations involved with this approach. You just go through with your situation as it is. If your meditation place is in a rich setting, just be in the midst of it. If it is in a simple setting, just be in the midst of that. You are not trying to get away from here to somewhere else. You are tuning in simply and directly to your process of life. This practice is the essence of here and now.

In this way, meditation becomes an actual part of life, rather than just a practice or exercise. It becomes inseparable from the instinct to live that accompanies all one's existence. That instinct to live can be seen as containing awareness, meditation, mindfulness. It constantly tunes us in to what is happening. So the life force that keeps us alive and that manifests itself continually in our stream of consciousness itself becomes the practice of mindfulness. Such mindfulness brings clarity, skill, and intelligence. Experience is brought from the framework of intense psychosomatic confusion into that of the real body, because we are simply tuning into what is *already* happening, instead of projecting anything further.

Since mindfulness is part of one's stream of consciousness, the practice of meditation cannot be regarded as something alien, as an emulation of some picturesque yogi who has a fixation on meditating all the time. Seen from the point of view of mindfulness of life, meditation is the total experience of any living being who has the instinct to survive. Therefore meditating—developing mindfulness—should not be regarded as a minority-group activity or as some specialized, eccentric pursuit. It is a worldwide approach that relates to all experience: it is tuning in to life.

We do not tune in as part of trying to live further. We do not approach mindfulness as a further elaboration of the survival instinct. Rather we just see the sense of survival as it is taking place in us already. You are here; you are living; let it be that way—that is mindfulness. Your heart pulsates and you breathe. All kinds of things are happening in you at once. Let mindfulness work with that, let that be mindfulness, let every beat of your heart, every breath, be mindfulness itself. You do not have to breathe specially; your breath *is* an expression of mindfulness. If you approach meditation in this way, it becomes very personal and very direct.

Having such an outlook and such a relationship with the practice of meditation brings enormous strength, enormous energy and power. But this only comes if one's relationship to the present situation is accurate. Otherwise there is no strength because we are apart from the energy of that situation. The accuracy of mindfulness, on the other hand, brings not only strength, but a sense of dignity and delight. This is simply because we are doing something that is applicable that very moment. And we are doing it without any implications or motives. It is direct and right on the point.

But again it is necessary to say, once you have that experience of the presence of life, don't hang onto it. Just touch and go. Touch that presence of life being lived, then go. You do not have to ignore it. "Go" does not mean that we have to turn our backs on the experience and shut ourselves off from it; it means just being in it without further analysis and without further reinforcement. Holding onto life, or trying to reassure oneself that it is so, has the sense of death rather than life. It is only because we have that sense of death that we want to make sure that we are alive. We would like to have an insurance policy. But if we feel that we *are* alive, that is good enough. We do not have to make sure that we actually do breathe, that we actually can be seen. We do not have to check to be sure we have a shadow. Just living is enough. If we don't stop to reassure ourselves, living becomes very clear-cut, very alive, and very precise.

So mindfulness here does not mean pushing oneself toward something or hanging onto something. It means allowing oneself to be there in the very moment of what is happening in one's living process and then letting go.

Mindfulness of Effort

The next foundation of mindfulness is mindfulness of effort. The idea of *effort* is apparently problematical. Effort would seem to be at odds with the sense of being that arises from mindfulness of body. Also, pushing of any kind does not have an obvious place in the touch-and-go technique of the mindfulness of life. In either case, deliberate, heavy-handed effort would seem to endanger the open precision of the process of mindfulness. Still we cannot expect proper mindfulness to develop without some kind of exertion on our part. Effort is necessary. But the Buddhist notion of *right effort* is quite different from conventional definitions of effort.

One kind of conventional effort is oriented purely toward the achievement of a result: there is a sense of struggle and pushing, which is egged on by the sense of a goal. Such effort picks up momentum and begins to thrive on its own speed, like the run of a roadrunner. Another approach to effort is fraught with a sense of tremendous meaningfulness: there is no sense of uplift or inspiration in the work. Instead there is a strong feeling of being dutiful. One just slogs along, slowly and surely, trying to chew through obligations in the manner of a worm in a tree. A worm just chews through whatever comes in front of its mouth; the channel that its belly passes through is its total space.

Neither of these kinds of effort has a sense of openness or precision. The traditional Buddhist analogy for right effort is the walk of an elephant or tortoise. The elephant moves along surely, unstoppably, with great dignity. Like the worm, it is not excitable, but unlike the worm, it has a panoramic view of the ground it is treading on. Though it is serious and slow, because of the elephant's ability to survey the ground there is a sense of playfulness and intelligence in its movement.

In the case of meditation, trying to develop an inspiration that is based on wanting to forget one's pain and on trying to make one's practice thrive on a sense of continual accomplishment is quite immature. On the other hand, too much solemnity and dutifulness creates a lifeless and narrow outlook and a stale psychological environment. The style of right effort, as taught by the Buddha, is serious but not *too* serious. It takes advantage of the natural flow of instinct to

bring the wandering mind constantly back to the mindfulness of breathing.

The crucial point in the bringing-back process is that it is
not necessary to go through deliberate stages: first preparing
to do it, then getting a hold on one's attention, then finally
dragging it back to the breathing as if we were trying to
drag a naughty child back from doing something terrible. It
is not a question of forcing the mind back to some particular
object, but of bringing it back down from the dream world
into reality. We are breathing, we are sitting. That is what
we are doing, and we should be doing it completely, fully,
wholeheartedly.

There is a kind of technique, or trick, here that is extremely effective and useful, not only for sitting meditation,
but also in daily life, or meditation-in-action. The way of
coming back is through what we might call the *abstract
watcher*. This watcher is just simple self-consciousness, without aim or goal. When we encounter anything, the first flash
that takes place is the bare sense of duality, of separateness.
On that basis, we begin to evaluate, pick and choose, make
decisions, execute our will. The abstract watcher is just the
basic sense of separateness—the plain cognition of being
there before any of the rest develops. Instead of condemning
this self-consciousness as dualistic, we take advantage of this
tendency in our psychological system and use it as the basis
of the mindfulness of effort. The experience is just a sudden
flash of the watcher's being there. At that point we don't
think, "I must get back to the breath" or "I must try and
get away from these thoughts." We don't have to entertain a
deliberate and logical movement of mind that repeats to itself the purpose of sitting practice. There is just suddenly a
general sense that something is happening here and now,
and we are brought back. Abruptly, immediately, without a
name, without the application of any kind of concept, we

have a quick glimpse of changing the tone. That is the core of the mindfulness of effort practice.

One of the reasons that ordinary effort becomes so dreary and stagnant is that our intention always develops a verbalization. Subconsciously, we actually verbalize: "I must go and help so-and-so because it is half-past one" or "This is a good thing for me to do; it is good for me to perform this duty." Any kind of sense of duty we might have is always verbalized, though the speed of conceptual mind is so great that we may not even notice the verbalization. Still, the contents of the verbalization are clearly felt. This verbalization pins the effort to a fixed frame of reference, which makes it extremely tiresome. In contrast, the abstract effort we are talking about flashes in a fraction of a second, without any name or any idea with it. It is just a jerk, a sudden change of course which does not define its destination. The rest of the effort is just like an elephant's walk—going slowly, step by step, observing the situation around us.

You could call this abstract self-consciousness *leap* if you like, or *jerk,* or *sudden reminder;* or you could call it *amazement.* Sometimes it could also be also felt as panic, unconditioned panic, because of the change of course—something comes to us and changes our whole course. If we work with this sudden jerk, and do so with no effort in the effort, then effort becomes self-existing. It stands on its own two feet, so to speak, rather than needing another effort to trigger it off. If the latter were the case, effort would have to be deliberately manufactured, which would run counter to the whole sense of meditation. Once you have had that sudden instant of mindfulness, the idea is not to try to maintain it. You should not hold onto it or try to cultivate it. Don't entertain the messenger. Don't nurse the reminder. Get back to meditation. Get into the message.

This kind of effort is extremely important. The sudden

flash is a key to all Buddhist meditation, from the level of basic mindfulness to the highest levels of tantra. Such mindfulness of effort could definitely be considered the most important aspect of mindfulness practice. Mindfulness of body creates the general setting; it brings meditation into the psychosomatic setup of one's life. Mindfulness of life makes meditation practice personal and intimate. Mindfulness of effort makes meditation workable: it connects the foundations of mindfulness to the path, to the spiritual journey. It is like the wheel of a chariot, which makes the connection between the chariot and the road, or like the oar of a boat. Mindfulness of effort actualizes the practice; it makes it move, proceed.

But we have a problem here. Mindfulness of effort cannot be deliberately manufactured; on the other hand, it is not enough just to hope that a flash will come to us and we will be reminded. We cannot just leave it up to "that thing" to happen to us. We have to set some kind of general alarm system, so to speak, or prepare a general atmosphere. There must be a background of discipline which sets the tone of the sitting practice. Effort is important on this level also; it is the sense of not having the faintest indulgence toward any form of entertainment. We have to give something up. Unless we give up our reservations about taking the practice seriously, it is virtually impossible to have that kind of instantaneous effort dawn on us. So it is extremely important to have respect for the practice, a sense of appreciation, and a willingness to work hard.

Once we do have a sense of commitment to relating with things as they actually are, we have opened the way to the flash that reminds us: *that, that, that.* "That what?" does not apply any more. Just *that,* which triggers an entirely new state of consciousness and brings us back automatically to mindfulness of breathing or a general sense of being.

We work hard at not being diverted into entertainment. Still, in some sense, we can enjoy the very boring situation of the practice of sitting meditation. We can actually appreciate not having lavish resources of entertainment available. Because of having already included our boredom and ennui, we have nothing to run away from and we feel completely secure and grounded.

This basic sense of appreciation is another aspect of the background that makes it possible for the spontaneous flash of the reminder to occur more easily. This is said to be like falling in love. When we are in love with someone, because our whole attitude is open toward that person somehow or other we get a sudden flash of that person—not as a name or as a concept of what the person looks like; those are afterthoughts. We get an abstract flash of our lover as *that.* A flash of *that* comes into our mind first. Then we might ponder on that flash, elaborate on it, enjoy our daydreams about it. But all this happens afterward. The flash is primal.

Openness always brings that kind of result. A traditional analogy is that of the hunter. The hunter does not have to think of a stag or a mountain goat or a bear or any specific animal; he is looking for *that.* When he walks and hears some sound, or senses some subtle possibility, he does not think of what animal he is going to find; just a feeling of *that* comes up. Anybody in any kind of complete involvement—on the level of the hunter, the lover, or the meditator—has the kind of openness that brings about sudden flashes. It is an almost magical sensation of thatness, without a name, without concept, without idea. This is the instant of effort, concentrated effort, and awareness follows after that. Having disowned that sudden experience, awareness very slowly comes and settles back to the earthy reality of just being there.

Mindfulness of Mind

Often mindfulness is referred to as *watchfulness*. But that should not give the impression that mindfulness means watching something happening. Mindfulness means *being* watchful, rather than watching some *thing*. This implies a process of intelligent alertness, rather than the mechanical business of simply observing what happens. Particularly the fourth foundation—mindfulness of mind—has qualities of an aroused intelligence operating. The intelligence of the fourth foundation is a sense of light-handedness. If you open the windows and doors of a room the right amount, you can maintain the interior feeling of roomness and, at the same time, have freshness from outside. Mindfulness of mind brings that same kind of intelligent balance.

Without mind and its conflicts, we could not meditate or develop balance, or develop anything at all for that matter. Therefore, conflicts that arise from mind are regarded as a necessary part of the process of mindfulness. But at the same time, those conflicts have to be controlled enough so that we can come back to our mindfulness of breathing. A balance has to be maintained. There has to be a certain discipline so that we are neither totally lost in daydream nor missing the freshness and openness that come from not holding our attention too tightly. This balance is a state of wakefulness, mindfulness.

People with different temperaments bring different approaches to the practice of meditation. Some people are extremely orthodox, in fact dictatorial, with themselves. Others are extraordinarily loose; they just hang out, so to speak, in the meditation posture and let everything happen. Other people struggle back and forth between those two extremes, not knowing exactly what to do. How one approaches the sitting situation will depend on one's moods and the type of person one is, obviously. But always a certain sense of accuracy is required, and a certain sense of freedom is required.

Mindfulness of mind means being with one's mind. When you sit and meditate, you are there: you are being with your body, with your sense of life or survival, with your sense of effort, and at the same time, you are being with your mind. You are being there. Mindfulness of mind suggests a sense of presence and a sense of accuracy in terms of being there. You are there, therefore you can't miss yourself. If you are not there, then you might miss yourself. But that also would be a doubletake: if you realize you are not there, that means you are there. That brings you back to where you are—back to square one.

The whole process is very simple, actually. Unfortunately, explaining the simplicity takes a lot of vocabulary, a lot of grammar. However, it is a very simple matter. And that matter concerns you and your world. Nothing else. It does not particularly concern enlightenment, and it does not particularly concern metaphysical comprehension. In fact, this simple matter does not particularly concern the next minute, or the minute before this one. It only concerns the very small area where we are now.

Really we operate on a very small basis. We think we are great, broadly significant, and that we cover a whole large area. We see ourselves as having a history and a future, and here we are in our big-deal present. But if we look at ourselves clearly in this very moment, we see we are just grains of sand—just little people concerned only with this little dot which is called *nowness.*

We can only operate on one dot at a time, and mindfulness of mind approaches our experience in that way. We are there and we approach ourselves on the very simple basis of *that.* *That* does not particularly have many dimensions, many perspectives; it is just a simple thing. Relating directly to this little dot of nowness is the right understanding of austerity. And if we work on this basis, it is possible to begin to see the truth of the matter, so to speak—to begin to see what nowness really means.

This experience is very revealing in that it is very personal. It is not personal in the sense of petty and mean. The idea is that this experience is *your* experience. You might be tempted to share it with somebody else, but then it becomes their experience, rather than what you wished for: your/their experience, jumbled together. You can never achieve that. People have different experiences of reality, which cannot be jumbled together. Invaders and dictators of all kinds have tried to make others have their experience, to make a big concoction of minds controlled by one person. But that is impossible. Everyone who has tried to make that kind of spiritual pizza has failed. So you have to accept that your experience is personal. The personal experience of nowness is very much there and very obviously there. You cannot even throw it away!

In sitting practice, or in the awareness practice of everyday life, for that matter, you are not trying to solve a wide array of problems. You are looking at one situation that is very limited. It is so limited that there is not even room to be claustrophobic. If it is not there, it is not there. You missed it. If it is there, it is there. That is the pinpoint of mindfulness of mind, that simplicity of total up-to-dateness, total directness. Mind functions singly. Once. And once. One thing at a time. The practice of mindfulness of mind is to be there with that one-shot perception, constantly. You get a complete picture from which nothing is missing: that is happening, now that is happening, now that is happening. There is no escape. Even if you focus yourself on escaping, that is also a one-shot movement of which you could be mindful. You can be mindful of your escape—of your sexual fantasy or your aggression fantasy.

Things always happen one at a time, in a direct, simple movement of mind. Therefore, in the technique of mindfulness of mind, it is traditionally recommended that you be aware of each single-shot perception of mind as thinking: "I am thinking I hear a sound." "I am thinking I smell a scent." "I am thinking I feel hot." "I am thinking I feel cold." Each one of these is a total approach to experience— very precise, very direct, one single movement of mind. Things always happen in that direct way.

Often we tend to think that we are very clever and we can get away from that direct nature of things. We feel we can get around that choiceless simplicity by approaching something from the back door—or from above, from the loft. We feel that we can prove ourselves to be extremely intelligent and resourceful that way. We are cunning and shifty. But somehow it does not work. When we think we are approaching something from the back door, we do not understand that it is an illusion that there is *something else* to approach. At that moment there is only the back-doorness. That one-shot back-doorness is the totality of what is. We *are* the back door. If we are approaching from the loft, you, me, everybody, all of us are up there. The whole thing is up there, rather than there being something else for us to go down and invade and control. There isn't anything else at all. It is a one-shot deal. That one-shot reality is all there is. Obviously we can make up an illusion. We can imagine that we are conquering the universe by multiplying ourselves into hundreds of aspects and personalities: the conquering and the conquered. But that is like the dream state of someone who is actually asleep. There is only the one shot; everything happens only once. There is just *that*. Therefore mindfulness of mind is applicable.

So meditation practice has to be approached in a very simple and very basic way. That seems to be the only way that it will apply to our experience of what we actually are. That way, we do not get into the illusion that we can function as a hundred people at once. When we lose the simplicity we begin to be concerned about ourselves: "While I'm doing this, such-and-such is going to happen. What shall I do?" Thinking that more than *that* is happening, we get involved in hope and fear in relation to all kinds of things that are not actually happening. Really it does not work that way. While we are doing *that*, we are doing that. If something else happens, we are doing something else. But two things cannot happen at once; it is impossible. It is easy to *imagine* that two things are happening at once, because our journey back and forth between the two may be very speedy. But even then we are doing only one thing at a time.

The idea of mindfulness of mind is to slow down the fickleness of jumping back and forth. We have to realize that we are not extraordinary mental acrobats. We are not all that well trained. And even an extraordinarily well-trained mind could not manage that many things at once—not even two. But because things are very simple and direct, we can focus on, be aware and mindful of, one thing at a time. That one-pointedness, that bare attention, seems to be the basic point.

It is necessary to take that logic all the way and realize that even to apply bare attention to what we are doing is impossible. If we try, we have two personalities: one personality is the bare attention; the other personality is doing things. Real bare attention is being there all at once. We do not apply bare attention *to* what we are doing; we are not mindful *of* what we are doing. That is impossible. Mindfulness is the act as well as the experience, happening at the same time. Obviously, we could have a somewhat dualistic attitude at the beginning, before we get into real mindfulness, that we are willing to be mindful, willing to surrender, willing to discipline ourselves. But then we do the thing; we just do it. It is like the famous Zen saying "When I eat, I eat; when I sleep, I sleep." You just do it, with absolutely no implication behind what you are doing, not even of mindfulness.

When we begin to feel implications of mindfulness, we are beginning to split ourselves. Then we are faced with our resistance, and hundreds of other things seemingly begin to attack us, to bother us. Trying to be mindful by deliberately looking at oneself involves too much watcher. Then we have lost the one-shot simplicity. Perhaps we could have a discussion.

STUDENT: I don't understand how *sem* works.

TRUNGPA RINPOCHE: Sem is basic mind. But instead of using the word *mind* as a noun, it might be more helpful to think of it as a verb, as in "minding one's business." Sem is an active process, because you cannot have mind without an object of mind. Mind and its object are one process. Mind only functions in relation to a reference point. In other words, you cannot see anything in the dark. The function of sight is to see something that is not darkness—to see an object, in the light. In the same way, the function of mind is to have a reference point, a relative reference point which survives the mind, the minding process. That is happening right now, actually, everywhere.

STUDENT: I was wondering if you could speak a little more about how mind, or "minding," creates the world. Are you talking about creating in the sense that if we are not mindful of the world the world does not exist? I feel you're saying something else besides that.

TRUNGPA RINPOCHE: Well, mind is very simple perception: it can only survive on "other." Otherwise it starves to death.

S: You mean the mind can only exist on things outside of itself?

TR: That is right. But there is also the possibility that mind can go too far in that direction. Mind cannot exist without the projection of a relative reference point; on the other hand, mind also cannot exist if it is too crowded with projections. That way it also loses its reference point. So mind has to maintain a certain balance. To begin with, mind looks for a way to secure its survival. It looks for a mate, a friend; it creates the world. But when it begins to get too crowded—too many connections, too much world— it rejects its projections; it creates a little niche somewhere and fights tooth and nail to maintain it in order to survive. Sometimes mind loses the game. It becomes psychotic, completely mad. You "lose your mind," as we say: you cannot even function on an ordinary logical level. Such psychosis results from either of the two extremes: you are completely overcrowded by the whole projection of the world or, on the other hand, you lack anything for mind to work with. So mind can only exist in the neurosis of relative reference, not in psychosis. When it reaches the psychotic level, mind ceases to function as mind. It becomes something else, something poisonous.

STUDENT: According to that model, how would meditation practice affect the relationship between mind and the world it's doing battle with?

TRUNGPA RINPOCHE: The purpose of meditation practice is to try to save oneself from psychosis.

S: But you still maintain the world? You still maintain the neurotic state, basically?

TR: Not that necessarily, either. There is an alternative mind that does not need the neurotic world. This is where the idea of enlightenment comes in. Enlightened mind can go further and further, beyond questions of relative reference. It does not have to keep up with this world. It reaches a point where it does not have to sharpen itself on this neurotic world any more. There is another level of experience which still has a reference point, but it is a reference point without demand, a reference point that does not need further reference points. That is called nonduality. This does not mean to say that you dissolve into the world or the world becomes you. It's not a question of oneness but rather a question of zeroness.

STUDENT: Rinpoche, how does the notion of mind that you've talked about relate to the notion of ego and the strategies of maintaining ego?

TRUNGPA RINPOCHE: Mind as we have been talking about it *is* ego. Ego can survive only in relation to a reference point, not by itself. But I am trying to make the whole thing quite simple and relate it directly to the practice of meditation. If we think practicing meditation is concerned with working with ego, that sounds like too big a deal. Whereas if we just work with mind, that is an actual, real thing to us. In order to wake up in the morning you have to know it is morning—there is light outside and you have awakened. Those simple things are a perfect example of basic ego. Ego survives and thrives on reference point. So sem is ego, yes.

STUDENT: You talked about mind relating to externals only. What do you consider it when the mind is functioning in pure intellection or imagination, creating its own object, so to speak.

TRUNGPA RINPOCHE: That is external.

S: But there could be nothing out there. You could be in a darkened cell imagining that you are hearing a symphony, for example; it exists only in your mind.

TR: Sure. That is outside. That seems to be the point. Maybe you are not really talking to me now. Maybe you are in a dark room and you are talking to your version of me. Somehow the physical visual situation is not that important a factor. Any mental object, mental content, is regarded as an external thing.

STUDENT: In regard to the technique of breathing, is there any particular reason why we identify with the outbreath rather than the inbreath?

TRUNGPA RINPOCHE: That's a question of openness. You have to create some kind of gap, some area where there is less strain. Once you breathe out, you're sure to breathe in again, so there's room for relief of some kind. Nothing needs watching there.

Also, outbreathing is an expression of stepping out of your centralized system. Outbreathing has nothing to do with centralizing in your body, where usually everything is psychosomatically bottled up. Instead, by identifying with the outbreath you are sharing, you are giving something out.

STUDENT: When you were talking about "flat-bottomed" ideas, you said that the flat bottom is what provides an openness, or a space, as opposed to having wings on your mind—flying thoughts or whatever. What makes the panic arise that made the retreatant you spoke of turn to her book, and that makes us run away from that sense of groundedness?

TRUNGPA RINPOCHE: A lot of fear comes when things

are too clearly defined. The situation becomes overwhelmingly sharp and direct and accurate, so that you would rather interpret it than simply acknowledge it. It is like when you say something very plain and direct to someone and you find him saying, "In other words, you are saying blah, blah, blah, blah, blah." Instead of relating directly to what has been said, he has a tendency to try to keep his twist. That seems to be a problem of shyness, of being shy of the bluntness of reality, of the "formness," the "thingness" that exists in our world and that nobody wants to face. Facing that is the highest form of sanity and enlightened vision. That seems to be the basic point of certain descriptions in *The Tibetan Book of the Dead*, where it describes a bright light coming toward you that you shy away from; you are frightened of it. Then there is a dull, seductive light coming from one of the six realms of neurotic existence, and you are attracted to that instead. You prefer the shadow to the reality. That is the kind of problem that exists. Often the reality is so blunt and outrageous and overwhelming that you feel facing it would be like sitting on a razor blade.

STUDENT: You spoke of experiencing the body. There are a lot of techniques and practices for feeling the body, where you focus attention on a physical sensation, tension, or whatever you feel when you attempt to feel the physical body. I'm wondering what relation that kind of practice has to the practice with the breath that you described. Are those techniques a different thing, or would they reinforce the practice with the breath?

TRUNGPA RINPOCHE: Your breath *is* your physical body from the point of view of this approach. There are all kinds of sensations that you experience along with the breath: pains, aches, itches, pleasurable feelings, and so on. You experience all those things along with the breath. Breath is the theme, and the other things go along with it. So the idea of the breathing technique is simply to be very precise about what you are experiencing. You relate to those sensations as they come up, along with your breath, without imagining that you are experiencing your body. Those experiences are not at all your body's experiences. That is impossible. Actually, you are in no way in a position to experience your body. Those experiences are just thoughts: "I'm thinking I'm in pain." It is the thought of pain, the thought of itch, and so forth.

S: So you are saying that the breathing technique is in a way a saner attitude than believing, "Now I'll feel my body" and making a project out of that?

TR: The breathing technique is a literal one, a direct one. It faces what is actually the case rather than just trying to turn out some result.

STUDENT: Before you were saying that when we are sitting here and taking notes, or focusing on the speaker and relaxing, we have a psychosomatic notion of body. And *psychosomatic,* the way I understand it, is sort of an imagined thing, or something that has to do with one's mind, with how the mind is affecting the body. Like when we say someone has a psychosomatic disease, it means their mind is having some effect on their body. How is that related to the fact that we're sitting here relaxing and listening to a speaker? How is that a psychosomatic sense of body?

TRUNGPA RINPOCHE: The point is that whatever we do in our lives, we don't actually just do it; we are affected by mind. Maybe the body, the true body, is being pressured by the psychosomatic speed of the mind. You might say that there is a possibility that you are sitting here now properly, in a nonpsychosomatic way. But still, the whole situation of sitting here was brought together, the whole incident was moved into place, by a psychosomatic driving force. So your sitting here was set up by the psychosomatic system, basically. If you have some kind of psychosomatic convulsion and you throw up—you actually do throw up stuff, which is not psychosomatic stuff but body stuff—it is nevertheless manifested in psychosomatic style. Its being thrown up was instigated by a psychosomatic process. That is the kind of situation we are in. Fundamentally our whole world is psychosomatic from that point of view. The whole process of living is composed of psychosomatic hangups. The desire to listen to the teachings comes from beginning to be aware of one's hangups. Since we have begun to be aware of our hangups we would like to create this further hangup to clear up the existing hangups.

S: Instead of relating directly?

TR: Well, one never does that until one has some kind of flash of something on the level of enlightenment. Until that point everything one does is always by innuendo.

S: So any kind of disease or anything that's affecting you is psychosomatic?

TR: It is not only disease that is psychosomatic. Your process of health is psychosomatic, already. Actually, disease is sort of an extra thing, like yeast growing on top of your back.

STUDENT: Rinpoche, with regard to touch-and-go, if a fantasy arises, to what point do you allow that fantasy to develop before you let go of it?

TRUNGPA RINPOCHE: Once it arises, that is already "touch." Then let it be as it is. Then it goes. There is a peak point there. First, there is creation of the fantasy; then it reaches maturity; then it is beyond its prime; and then it slowly vanishes or tries to turn into something else.

S: Sometimes a fantasy will turn into a whole emotional plot which seems to get more and more complex.

TR: That is beating a dead horse. You just let it come, let it play out its impetus or energy, then just let it go. You have to taste it, then let it go. Having tasted it, it is not recommended to manipulate it any further.

S: When you speak of touch-and-go, evidently meditating, sitting practice, is the "touch." Do you mean that there are also times when it's inappropriate to be mindful in this manner? That in everyday life we should just let mindfulness go?

TR: I think there is some misunderstanding there. "Touch" and "go" always come together. It is like whenever there is a one, there is a zero. The number series, starting with one, implies zero. Numbers do not make sense if there is no such thing as zero. "Touch" has no meaning without "go." They are simultaneous. That simultaneity is mindfulness, which happens during both formal sitting practice and the post-meditation experience of everyday life.

STUDENT: Previously you mentioned the retreatant who had the feeling of sitting on a razor blade when things became very clear, very distinct. Could you relate that experience to the sense of delight in the mindfulness of life?

TRUNGPA RINPOCHE: It is the same experience, actually. Whenever there is a threat of death, that also brings a sense of life. It is like taking a pill because you fear that otherwise you might die. The pill is associated with the threat of death, but you take it with the attitude that it will enable you to live. Facing the moment clearly is like taking that pill: there is a fear of death and a love of life simultaneously.

STUDENT: How does mindfulness of life inform ethical behavior, ethical action?

TRUNGPA RINPOCHE: Things are done without mindfulness in the samsaric world; we thrive on that. Consequently, almost everything we do is somewhat disjointed: somehow things don't click, they don't fit; there is something illogical about our whole approach. We might be very reasonable, good people; still, behind the facade we are somewhat off. There is fundamental neurosis taking place all the time on our part, which in turn creates pain for other people as well as ourselves. People get hurt by that, and their reactions create more of the same. That is what we call the neurotic world, or samsara. Nobody is actually having a good time. Even ostensibly good times are somewhat pushed. And the undercurrent of frustration from sensing that creates further indulgence.

Mindfulness of life is an entirely different approach, in which life is treated as precious, which is to say, mindfully. Things are seen in their own right rather than as aspects of the vicious cycle of neurosis. Everything is jointed rather than disjointed. One's state of mind becomes coherent, so there is a basic workability concerning how to conduct one's life, in a general sense. One begins to become literate in reading the style of the world, the pattern of the world. That is just the starting point; it is by no means the final stage. It is just the beginning of seeing how to read the world.

STUDENT: I really cannot imagine what experience would be like without all kinds of imagination and projections. I can't get a sense of what it would be like to participate in the world just as it is, just as things are occurring and coming up.

TRUNGPA RINPOCHE: Are you interested in finding out?

S: I guess so.

TR: Well, it is very hard to do. The reason it is hard is

that you are doing it. It is like looking for a lost horse. In order to look for it, you need to ride your lost horse. On the other hand, maybe you are riding on your lost horse, but still you are looking for it. It is something like that. It's one of those.

You see, there is really no such thing as ultimate reality. If there was such a thing, for that reason alone that could not be it. That is the problem. So you are back to square one. And the only thing, it seems, that you can do is to practice. That is good enough.

STUDENT: In connection with the flash of waking up, in mindfulness of effort, I still don't clearly understand where you are supposed to come back from and what you are supposed to come back to.

TRUNGPA RINPOCHE: Once that flash happens, you do not have to find out and appreciate where you came from. That is what I mean by, "Don't entertain the messenger." You also do not need an idea of where you are going. After the flash, your awareness is like a snowflake released from the clouds. It is going to settle down to the ground anyway. You have no choice.

STUDENT: Sometimes being mindful of the exhalation seems to become too deliberate. It seems too much that the watcher is doing it from above, rather than the breathing and the mindfulness being simultaneous.

TRUNGPA RINPOCHE: The touch-and-go approach is applicable here. You touch the exhalation and then disown the awareness even of that. If you are trying to have bare attention constantly, then you have a problem of being very rigid and dragging yourself along. So you touch with the breath and go with the breath. That way there is a sense of freshness, a change of air. It is like a pulsation, or like listening to a musical beat. If you are trying to keep with one beat you miss another. But if you touch and go you begin to hear the rhythm; and then you hear the entirety of the music, too. Another example is eating food: when you eat food you don't taste it constantly, just now and then. It is the same way with any experience. We hover around our interest. Always we just touch the highlights of our interest. So the touch-and-go style of mindfulness practice is borrowed from the basic style of mind. If you go along with that, then there is no problem at all.

STUDENT: I somewhat understand how mindfulness of mind is a one-shot movement. But then if effort comes in, that no longer seems simultaneous or spontaneous.

TRUNGPA RINPOCHE: Effort comes in off and on—at the beginning, during, and at the end. For instance, you are holding that microphone because you had an interest in asking a question. Now while you are listening to the answer, you have forgotten that you are holding the microphone, but that original effort is still hanging over. You are still holding it, not dropping it. So a lot of journeys back and forth take place with one's effort, rather than its being maintained constantly. Therefore you do not have to strain and push constantly. If you do, there is no practice, no meditation; the whole thing just becomes a big deal of effort. Shifting, alternating constantly, creates the space of meditation. If you are one hundred percent effortful, you blow the whole thing. There is nothing left but a tense lump of muscle sitting in the middle of a field. This happens all the time in life situations. It is like trying to knead dough. If you knead too hard you won't have any dough left in your hand—you will just be pushing you hand against the board. But if you have the feeling that the purpose of kneading hard is to work with the dough, then you have some compromises taking place, some intelligence coming into play. Without that, effort alone just kills.

STUDENT: Without exercising some kind of incredible deliberateness, my entire meditation practice seems to be fantasy. There seems to be hardly any time that I am relating with my breath. I am basically just sitting there daydreaming or else very deliberately, heavy-handedly trying to relate with my breath.

TRUNGPA RINPOCHE: Well, go and sit.

S: What should I do when I sit?

TR: Sit.

S: That's all? What about working with my breath?

TR: Sit. Go ahead and sit. Just go ahead and do it.

4

Devotion

"The devotional relationship between student and master becomes a living analogy for the student's relationship to life in general. Over a period of time this relationship works through many layers of unauthentic communication, based on ever more subtle deceptions of ego. The result for the student can be a totally clear and unencumbered relationship to his or her world."

Devotion, in the conventional sense, is a feeling of trust. The object of devotion, whether a person or an idea, is felt to be trustworthy and definite, more solid and real than oneself. In comparison, the devotee feels himself to be somewhat uncertain, not solid or full enough. He feels he lacks something, and this is the reason for his devotion toward somebody or something else. He feels inadequate standing on his own two feet, so he turns elsewhere for advice, security, or warmth. This type of devotion can be directed toward any number of ideas, or it can be directed toward our parents, our school teachers, our spiritual teacher, our bank manager, our wife or husband—toward whomever seems to have achieved life's goal in the conventional sense, which

Based on "The True Meaning of Devotion," Barnet, Vermont, 1973.

perhaps means anyone who has accumulated a lot of experience or information.

In general, the character of devotion seems to depend on the manner in which we relate the quality of trust or sanity within ourselves to something outside us. In the tradition of Buddhism, devotion to a teacher or master plays an extremely important role. Although, like conventional devotion, it may in the beginning be based on a sense of inadequacy and a wish to flee that inadequacy rather than to face and work with it, it goes far beyond that point. The devotional relationship between student and master becomes a living analogy for the student's relationship to life in general. Over a period of time this relationship works through many layers of inauthentic communication, based on ever more subtle deceptions of ego. The result for the student can be a totally clear and unencumbered relationship to his or her world. What makes the student persist in this long, difficult, and often extremely painful voyage of discovery is his or her devotion to the teacher—the conviction that the teacher indeed embodies the truth of his teaching. Throughout its various levels of development, devotion can be seen as having two aspects: admiration and absence of arrogance.

Admiration may be construed as hero worship. We look up to people who have a great deal of talent and dignity. We may idolize such people, hoping to make them part of us, to incorporate them into our territory. We hope in this way to participate in their greatness.

On the other hand, seeing talented people and their fine creations may make us jealous and depressed. We could feel we are too stupid and incompetent to compete with such tremendous discipline and talent. We might find ourselves actually resentful toward someone who is beautiful or polished. We may even experience their existence and their accomplishments as a hurt. Fine accomplishments or works of beauty may be such a threat that something in us would almost like to destroy them, to burn down all the art museums. At the very least we would like to insult those people who are more talented than we are. This is hero hatred, which is another version of hero worship.

A third possibility is that we may feel a really immense distance between the great and talented people and ourselves. We may feel that their accomplishments are splendid, but that they have nothing to do with us because they are so far above us. This attitude permits us to avoid being pained by a comparison with such accomplished people. With this attitude, we seal ourselves off completely.

The hidden assumption of this approach, whether in the form of adoration, hatred, or aloofness, is that there are heroes and there are incompetents, and we are among the incompetents. A separation is maintained.

In relating to a spiritual teacher, admiration is usually expressed in one of those three neurotic styles. In the case of seductive admiration, we want to consume the teacher completely so that he or she becomes part of us; in that case, we obliterate the actual features of the relationship under a thick layer of honey. In the repelling style of admiration, we are so overcome by awe and fear that, although we cannot help still being involved with the teacher, we keep the teacher in such a lofty niche that the possibility of direct appreciation is completely closed off. No matter what our style, it is usual to try to strategize our devotion so that the guru is not a threat.

A combination of these styles was visible in the fad that developed in the early part of this decade, when gurus were related to as popular idols or good luck charms. Young people completely covered their walls with pictures of spiritual superstars: gurus from India and Japan, American Indians, Eskimos, Tibetans—pinups of all kinds. In this way they could consider themselves on the good side of all sorts of great beings or great concepts. By relating to teachers as icons, they could express their admiration safely, without any danger of uncomfortable feedback.

Real admiration is much more direct than these contrived attitudes, and therefore it is more dangerous. Real admiration is based on a sense of courage and tremendous dignity. When we admire someone in a real way, we are not competing with that person or trying to win him over, but we are sharing his immense vision. The relationship can be a great celebration, because we do not approach it with a personal investment in any strategy or cause. In such admiration, our role is simply to devote ourselves completely, just to travel along without expecting anything in return for our admiration.

True admiration has clarity and bite. It is like breathing mountain air in winter, which is so cold and clear that we are afraid that it may freeze our lungs. Between breaths we may want to run into the cabin and throw a blanket over our heads lest we catch cold—but in true admiration we do not do that. Although the mountain air is threateningly clear as well as fantastically invigorating, we just breathe, without trying either to protect ourselves or to trap the air and take it with us. Like the mountains we are simply a part of that briskness: that is proper admiration or sharing.

The second quality of devotion is absence of arrogance. The arrogant approach is to be so passionately involved with our teacher that we become devotional chauvinists and cease to see the rest of the world properly. In fact, we become passionately involved with our own arrogance. We indulge our "devotion" by collecting information, techniques, stories, little words of wisdom—all to confirm our chauvinistic view. It actually reaches a point that the teacher upon whom our arrogance is based himself becomes a threat. The absurdity is that we even end up wanting to use our collection of ammunition against our teacher when he begins giving our "devotion" a hard time.

If our devotion is without arrogance there is not this resentment toward the world or the guru. Absence of such arrogance is absolutely necessary. When courting a teacher, students frequently make a sort of detailed application, listing all their insights and spiritual credentials. That is too arrogant; it is phony, out of the question altogether. It is fine to offer our particular skills or neuroses to the guru as a gift or an opening gesture. But if we begin to dress up our neuroses as virtues, like a person writing a resumé, that is unacceptable. Devotion without arrogance demands that we stop clinging to our particular case history, that we relate to the teacher and to the world in a naked and direct way, without hiding behind credentials.

Buddhism has three levels of development: *hinayana; mahayana;* and *vajrayana,* or *tantra.* Initially, at the hinayana level, devotion is very definite and very direct. The formula of devotion is what is known as *taking refuge.* One takes refuge in the Buddha as an example; in the dharma, or teaching, as a way of life; and in the sangha, or fellowhip of practitioners, as companionship.

At this level the inspiration for devotion arises from a sense of being trapped in the whirlpool of samsara—of being filled with pain, dissatisfaction, and neurosis. Not only are we in that state but there is the further frustration that however much we try to get out of that state, our too-speedy, too-desperate attempts only make our situation more hopeless. The traditional analogy for this is that of an elephant who feels very hot in the tropical sun and, wanting to bathe in some cool water, jumps into a mud hole. The more he moves around the more he sinks. At the beginning it seems very pleasurable, but when two-thirds of his body has sunk into the mud he begins to panic. He struggles more and more to get out, but it is too late.

Like the elephant, we try to rescue ourselves from our frustration, but the more we try to pull ourselves out the more we sink in. We feel completely helpless. It sometimes reaches the point of feeling that we have made a complete mess out of our lives. What are we to do if we do not get what we want? What are we to do when we have already gotten what we wanted? Even if we have had some success, what are we to do when things still go on after that? We are always back at square one. Our master plan has cheated us. There seems to be no alternative to frustration and confusion. It is this situation that is the inspiration to take refuge. At some point, instead of merely trying to struggle within ourselves, we feel that perhaps we ought to look around and try to find someone to rescue us. Taking refuge in the Buddha as an example means identifying with a person who was able in one lifetime to attain enlightenment and save himself. Since somebody has already done it, perhaps we could do the same thing.

Since we are in an emergency situation, the first thing we learn is that our struggle to pull ourselves out of samsara has to be given up. Being engaged in a struggle may give us some sense of security, in that at least we feel we are doing something. But that struggle has become useless and irrelevant: it only makes things worse. However, the pain we have experienced in our struggle cannot be forgotten. We have to work with it. Rather than struggling to escape pain, we have to make it our path. It then becomes a rich resource for learning. Relating to our pain in this manner is taking refuge in the dharma.

The sangha is composed of the people who follow such a path. We respect those who have undertaken the journey—those who have been able to get out of the mud—as well as our companions, who are working like ourselves. It is not a matter of leaning on others to avoid facing our loneliness. Rather, by taking refuge in the sangha, we acknowledge our aloneness, which in turn becomes an inspiration to others. The hinayana approach to devotion is not directed toward attaining a sense of emotional security. It is purely a response to an emergency. If we have been hurt in a car accident, we need an ambulance to take us to the hospital. When such an emergency arises, the hypothetical comforts of a successful journey are remote. The only thing we need is for the ambulance to come and fetch us. It is very alarming; we are completely stuck. So devotion in the hinayana is based on the desire to be rescued from the hopeless and chaotic situation in which we seem to dwell continually.

It should be clear at this point that those who become involved with the teaching in this way are quite different from spiritual shoppers who have the luxury of drifting from one involvement to another. For those who are really engaged in working on themselves, there is no time to shop around. They are simply concerned with getting some basic treatment. They have no time for philosophizing or analysis: they are stuck. Help is desperately needed because the pain is so intense.

Psychologically, there seems to be a basic difference in honesty between the hinayana practitioner, who acknowledges the urgent need for a rescuer, and the dilettante spiritual shopper. Spiritual shoppers might acknowledge that there is a problem, but they feel the problem can be patched over until they can get service to their liking. Spiritual shopping is a naive and simplistic version of the fantastic project of spiritual materialism—a project which simply creates and perpetuates suffering in its attempt to achieve egohood. Spiritual shoppers are looking for entertainment from spiritual teachings. In such an approach devotion is nonexistent. Of course, if such shoppers visit a store where the salesman has a tremendous personality and his merchandise is also fantastically good, they might momentarily feel overwhelming trust of some kind. But their basic attitude is not desperate enough. Their desperation has been concealed or patched over, so they make no real connection with the teaching. However, their patchwork is bound to fall apart, and in the midst of that chaos they will have no choice but to come to terms with their desperation. That is the point of emergency out of which the rudiments of genuine devotion arise. Desperation becomes very straightforward.

But what happens after we already have been treated for our pain—when our basic problems have been dealt with and we can afford to relax a little bit? Although our initial symptoms have been cured, our particular medical service may now appear not to be totally ideal, and we may begin to look for a better one. We can once again afford the luxury of shopping for the last word in spirituality, and devotion may be forgotten. We may even begin to develop a sense of resentment toward our teacher, feeling that he has interfered in our business and undermined our dignity. Once we have regained our strength—or hypocrisy—we tend to forget the kindness and generosity of the rescuer, and the compassionate acts he performed. Now that we are no longer stupid, unworthy persons looking for a rescuer, we may feel resentful of having been seen in that abject position. At that point, there is a need for eye-level communication, for a friend rather than a teacher. But how do we bridge the gap between the notion of a rescuer and that of a spiritual friend?

On the hinayana level our condition was similar to that of a patient in an emergency room. There was no point then in being personally introduced to the physician or in trying to be polite. However, when we have recovered from our operation there is the possibility that the person who performed the operation may take a further interest in us because he has learned a great deal about us during the course of our treatment. He also happens to like us tremendously. But there is the difficulty that as we recover we may resent his interest. We do not want to be intimidated by having our case history recalled.

At that point it is very hard to make a connection, but it is absolutely necessary. It is not like ordinary medical practice in which the doctor can transfer our case to someone else. The person we ran into in the emergency room has to carry on with us until real, fundamental, basic sanity has developed.

Now the notion of surrendering is very important. The greatest gift we can make is to open and expose ourselves. We have to show our physician our secret ailments. Still, the physician keeps calm and quiet and goes on liking us, however repulsive our secret ailments may be. So our relationship with the physician is ongoing.

So the second stage of devotion, on the level of mahayana, comes from discovering our teacher as a spiritual friend, or *kalyanamitra* in Sanskrit. The guru becomes a friend with whom we can communicate completely in the sense of communication between equals. But at the same time this particular friend is rather heavy-handed: he minds our business.

On the mahayana level, devotion is based on the feeling that we are, up to a point, worthy persons capable of receiving the teachings. Our inspiration, insights, pain, and neuroses all constitute us as good vessels. Our neuroses and pain are not regarded as bad, nor, for that matter, are our virtues regarded as good. Both are just the substance of the vessel. There is an overall sense of trust—a sense of warmth and compassion toward ourselves in that all our aspects can be included in the relationship with the spiritual friend. And devotion to the spiritual friend is complementary to that development of trust in ourselves: devotion at this point is no longer directed toward an external object alone. This attitude of nonaggression toward oneself and others is central to the *bodhisattva path*, which is at the heart of mahayana Buddhism.

Aggression manifests toward others as pride and toward oneself as depression. If we get fixated in either of these extremes we become unsuitable vessels for the teachings. The arrogant student is like a container turned upside-down; he is completely unreceptive to anything coming from outside himself. And the depressed student is like a container with holes in it; since he feels nothing will help he does not heed anything. It is not that before forming a relationship with a spiritual friend we have to become ideal vessels. That would be impossible. But if we have an occasional glimpse of that attitude of nonaggression—a positive attitude toward ourselves, without arrogance or pride—then that creates the possibility of our spiritual friend communicating with us directly.

The first obstacle to devotion at this point is negativity toward ourselves; we judge ourselves too harshly. The usual response to depression, to feeling unworthy of the teachings, is to try to change completely, by making a one-hundred-percent improvement. We set up a kind of totalitarian regime with the aim of making ourselves into perfect individuals without any faults whatsoever. Whenever we begin to notice our faults peeking through, our automatic reaction is to feel that our journey is being delayed and our perfection challenged. So we try to prune ourselves. We are willing to impose all sorts of discipline on ourselves, punishing our bodies and our minds. We inflict pain on ourselves through stringent rules of all kinds. We may go so far as to seek some magical cure for our shortcomings, since in moments of clarity we realize we cannot handle ourselves. This totalitarian approach seems to be falling once more into the pitfall of spiritual materialism, of trying to make oneself perfect.

The second obstacle to devotion is a further form of arrogance. The student may have received some glimpse of the teachings, and some preliminary sanity may have already developed in him, but then he starts taking liberties. He has too much trust in his own home-brewed potion, too much trust in do-it-yourself projects: "I have developed myself to this level, and I have achieved a lot of the things that I wanted to achieve. I'm sure that I don't have to go through the embarrassment of regarding someone as my spiritual friend any more. I can study the appropriate books and learn how to brew the spiritual medicines myself."

It is true than in some sense Buddhism can be described as a do-it-yourself process. The Buddha himself said, "Work out your own salvation with diligence." So it seems clear that, to a certain extent, salvation is up to us and we cannot really get help from outside. There is no magical gimmick that will solve our problems for us without pain. But while there is no possibility that such external magic or divine powers will save us, a spiritual friend is still necessary. Such a friend might only tell us that doing it ourselves is the only way, but we have to have someone to encourage us to do that and to show us that it can be done. Our friend has done it himself, and his predecessors in his spiritual lineage have done it as well. We have to have this proof that the spiritual path is not a gigantic hoax but a real thing, and that there *is* someone who can pass on the message, the understanding, the techniques. And it is necessary that this friend be a human being, not an abstract figure that can be manipulated by our wishful thinking; he is someone who shares the human condition with us and who works with us on that level. He must have a direct and very concrete understanding of us personally in order for there to be a proper connection.

Without that, we are unable to receive any real teachings, any real benefit.

In relating to the spiritual friend, at the same time that we trust ourselves and consider ourselves worthy vessels, there should also be some sense of hopelessness. At this point hopelessness does not mean despair, but simply a loss of interest in manufacturing further expectations. Ordinarily, we live in our world of expectations, which we embellish constantly. Hopelessness means being willing to live nakedly in the moment, without the reference point of our expectations. Expecting good fortune or bad fortune is like believing in fortune cookies: it is just entertaining ourselves with expectations. Chaos might arise or development and creativity might arise—either situation is possible—but in communicating with a spiritual friend we are not looking ahead; we are directly involved in the very moment. The spiritual friend does not exist as a dream of the future, like an arranged marriage that is yet to be consummated. The spiritual friend is right there in front of us—six inches away. He is right there. Whatever image we present to such a friend is immediately reflected back to us. That is why the spiritual friend is referred to as heavy-handed: he minds our business. He has no shyness of himself or us. Just being right there, he minds our business totally.

We cannot tread the path of mahayana without a spiritual friend—absolutely not—because we have to receive the good news of the bodhisattva's wide-open path. The spiritual friend both is and conveys that good news. He makes it possible to know the teachings and the practice as real, rather than purely as a myth to accept on the basis of blind faith. We have a tendency to look for miracles and magic as solutions to our problems. One reason for this is that we do not believe what we have been told concerning the hard facts of spirituality, and we actually regard the whole thing as a fable. We are so bored with living on this earth, we would like to go to the moon or to Mars, or to explore other solar systems. We do not want to believe that dealing with our situation happens right here; this place seems to be too small, too unexciting, too polluted and unclean. But the spiritual friend does not offer us any magical solution, any escape from our boredom. He relates to us on a very mundane level, right here on earth. While he does not perform miracles or magic, we see that he belongs to a lineage of generations and generations of teachers who have achieved complete openness. He provides proof of the teachings by acting as an example.

In this sense the spiritual friend is like a good baker in a lineage of bakers. The earliest bakers passed on their secrets for making good bread, from generation to generation. The present baker also bakes good bread and feeds it to us. The loaf he gives us to sample was not preserved through the generations as an antique; it is not a museum piece. This loaf has been baked fresh and is now hot, wholesome, and nourishing. It is an example of what freshness can be. The knowledge that has been handed down to us through the spiritual lineage has the same qualities. We can make an immediate connection with the spiritual friend and understand that in the past generations of teachers and students also experienced such a fresh and direct relationship.

The spiritual friend has real, living teachings, and we can relate with him thoroughly and completely. If we are simple and straightforward with him, neither condemning nor aggrandizing ourselves, then instead of blind faith, we begin to develop real devotion. We are convinced that something is happening—something that could make life completely workable—but at the same time we are not expecting anything extraordinary. So the relationship with the spiritual friend is very ordinary; it is communication on the level of our day-to-day living situation.

Our relationship with a spiritual friend tends to become even more demanding and much more energy consuming as we develop on the path. From the standpoint of fundamental devotion the sense of friendship is simply an appetizer. The true meaning of devotion manifests on the vajrayana level alone.

At the hinayana level our devotion was conditioned by our sense of desperation, and at the mahayana level it was conditioned by our loneliness. Only at the vajrayana level is there unconditioned devotion. At this level the relationship between student and teacher is very dangerous—but also extremely powerful. Finally, at this level, it could be described as a magical relationship.

When we reach the third stage of the Buddhist path—the vajrayana, or the stage of tantra—devotion brings with it an increased sense of its appropriate expression through action, particularly through what is known as *surrendering,* or *offering.* Such surrendering takes a great deal of effort and energy. Before discussing the vajrayana, we need to understand this notion of surrendering.

Usually we do not give merely for the sake of giving. We may give because we want to get rid of something, in which case it is like throwing it into a garbage pail. Or we may give at required times, such as at Christmas or on birthdays. Sometimes we give to express our appreciation to someone who has given us something, such as love, education, or support. Or we may use a gift to try to win somebody over. But we never seem to give in the absence of some purpose or scheme. We do not just give things—just like that.

Even at the mahayana level, generosity has a scheme to it, in that it is regarded as an act of letting go and has the purpose of learning the generosity that does not expect anything in return. Only at the vajrayana level does even that kind of scheme disappear and the total simplicity of just giving become possible. That type of giving may not seem to be very practical. From an ordinary business point of view, it is like throwing money down the drain; we could go so far as to say that it is insane to do such a thing. In this type of generosity we are not giving to prove how wealthy we are, or how visionary, but we are just giving everything—body, speech, and mind. In other words, we are giving the giver, so there ceases even to be a gift. It is just letting go.

Naturally, we would always like to watch the receiver of the gift appreciating what has been received. If we give our whole being and somebody thanks us for it, then we have not actually given it completely; we have gotten it back. We thrive on such confirmation. We do not want to just give, not knowing whether or not we will have ourselves with us any more. That is a terrible thought: if we give completely and hold nothing back we cannot even watch the process of giving; we cannot take part in that ritual. Losing ourselves is such a terrible idea that we would not even like to give up our anger or passion, because even such neuroses produce some kind of security. They may be painful, but they still serve to make the statement "I do exist."

We might say that just giving is asking too much; it definitely is. That is why it is important. Giving without concept is what makes room for the awakened state to be experienced. This cannot take place as a business deal. We cannot possess the dharma and deposit it in the bank. When we actually receive the teachings properly, there is nobody home to receive anything; there is no one to reap a profit. The teachings simply become a part of us, part of our basic being. The dharma cannot be owned as property or adornment.

The approach of ego at this level is to collect initiations

and teachers as ornaments: "I received millions of ordinations and trillions of initiations. I am completely soaked in blessings." That is the most decadent way of relating to the teachings, the most blatant form of spiritual materialism. In that approach we use the teaching and the teachers as part of ego's conspiracy to adorn itself, and thus we fall deeper and deeper asleep rather than opening up to anything. We become beggarly mystical egomaniacs.

Such attempts to strategize giving or to use the teachings for personal gain have to be given up completely at the vajrayana level. There is no longer room for the conditioned devotion of the hinayana and mahayana. At this level total generosity, or surrendering, is required; otherwise the meeting of minds between the teacher and student through which transmission takes place is impossible.

In vajrayana Buddhism the process of surrendering is catalyzed through what are known as the *four preliminary practices:* one hundred thousand prostrations; one hundred thousand repetitions of the refuge formula; one hundred thousand repetitions of a purifying mantra; and one hundred thousand symbolic offerings of one's body, speech, and mind and the whole universe to the guru. It should be noted that we cannot embark immediately on the vajrayana approach without first going through the hinayana and mahayana. Without that preparation, these preliminary practices tend to be ineffectual, because we do not actually give up anything through them. We merely go through the motions of surrendering, performing the gymnastics of a hundred thousand prostrations and playing with our spiritual gadgets. So unless we have started from the beginning with the disciplined meditation practice of the hinayana and the expansiveness and openness of the mahayana, we are unable to receive real empowerment and real transmission through the vajrayana tradition.

We initially related to the teacher as our rescuer; later he became a spiritual friend who engaged us in very intense communication. Now, in the vajrayana, the guru, or *vajra master,* begins to demand this further surrendering. At first we feel we have already done our giving away and trusting, and that we do not have anything more to surrender. We have already paid our dues and therefore we are worthy of the vajrayana teachings. At the beginning of the path we were in bad shape, and we surrendered ourselves to the physician in the emergency room; later, when we began to recover, we felt lonely and sought companionship. Now we feel we have already done everything we wanted to do: we have thrown everything overboard and surrendered our egos. But there is still something that needs to be surrendered, which is our collection of pride in the pain that we have already gone through. We have surrendered, but in the process of surrendering we have collected credentials, which are an obstacle. We have become respectable surrenderers who have carefully donated a certain chunk of their body, speech, mind, and energy. But something more is needed: complete surrender, complete humiliation, so to speak. And such devotion is possible only with the aid of a real friend.

In the beginning of the vajrayana one takes what is known as the *samaya* vow. A samaya vow is a bond that one establishes with one's teacher—a bond between oneself, one's teacher, and the teacher's lineage. To create a samaya bond it is not enough just to get up and do it. If we wanted to get married we could run off and have a quick ceremony before a justice of the peace, without having our parents' acknowledgment or even a good wedding feast, but the meaning and purpose of the marriage would be lost because there was no big deal. We just wanted to glue ourselves to somebody else. In the case of the samaya vow, a real marriage takes place between oneself, one's teacher, and the lineage. That is

why there is a tremendous need for surrendering and opening. It is absolutely necessary because of the demand that
that marriage makes on us.

As soon as the student drinks the water of the samaya
oath the water turns into the elixir of life, or *amrita,* which
sustains the student's conviction and remains in his heart.
But the surrendering process can also have deathly consequences. If the student has any trace of doubt or confusion
or deceit, the water turns into molten iron and destroys
him, carrying him to what is known as *vajra hell.* So samaya
is a very heavy commitment. It is extremely potent and
powerful. I personally feel that introducing the vajrayana
outright, in a country whose citizens have no idea of how
dangerous a step it is, is taking advantage of people's weakness. Collecting hundreds of thousands of candidates for
vajra hell seems to be uncompassionate, even if there are all
kinds of gadgets and excitement for them along the way.

In order to prepare suitable tantric students, we must
start with all sorts of warnings. Such warnings are absolutely
necessary. There is a traditional story about Indian merchants who sailed out onto the ocean to collect pearls. One
merchant who had a large ship gathered together a number
of people who wanted to go along on the venture. Attached
to the ship were four anchors. When it came time to sail
each day he would cut away one anchor with a warning: "Are
you sure you want to go through with this?" Only on the
fourth day did he set sail. Similarly, in order to launch
vajrayana in America, we must give repeated warnings about
the dangers of tantric practice. Of course, if we get out on
the ocean and collect beautiful pearls, it will be a fantastic
thing, an extraordinary situation. But suppose we are unable
to do that; suppose the participants are just blindly latching
on to the big businessman who owns the ship? That would
be disastrous, so there must be constant warnings.

In tantra, the guru is regarded as absolutely essential. He is the central figure for all the teachings. Without the guru we cannot transmute the water of the oath into elixir. To relate to the guru we need a tremendous amount of openness and surrendering—real surrendering, not surrendering with an ulterior motive, like that of the shopper who butters up the salesman because he wants his merchandise.

At first, this surrendering involves the body; we surrender the feeling that our body is a cozy nest—that if we go mad at least we will have something to relate to, which is our body. When we surrender our body to the guru we are surrendering our primal reference point. One's body becomes the possession of the lineage; it is not ours anymore. I am not talking here of becoming hysterical and losing sense consciousness; I mean that, surrendering one's body, psychologically one's dear life is turned over to somebody else. We do not have our dear life to hold onto any more. At the second stage of tantra, speech, which is the emotional level, is also surrendered. Our emotional security is no longer regarded as necessary or relevant. That need also is surrendered to the teachings and to the lineage as represented by the guru. The third stage involves the mind, the registering mechanism that exists in one's state of consciousness. The mind is also surrendered, so that we no longer have our logical intellectual games to cling to.

Finally everything is surrendered: body, speech, and mind. However, this does not mean that we become zombies or jellyfish. Such surrendering is a continual process rather than a one-shot suicidal affair, and the uncompromising intelligence that has emerged through our surrendering remains active and, through the surrendering process, becomes progressively more free.

Such a surrendering process and the demands that the tantric lineage make on the student might be described as outrageous, unlawful, or criminal. From the viewpoint of maintaining ego's kingdom, it is criminal. It is the final and ultimate way to uproot this thing that we try so hard to hold onto. It is absolutely terrible, even deathly. But such surrendering is a necessary part of opening.

At this point it could be said that we worship the guru—but not as a purely chauvinistic person to whom we have to surrender. That is the wrong frame of reference completely. He is not a dharma chauvinist: there is no chauvinism involved. Rather, the guru is a spokesman, ambassador, executioner, and policeman of openness, and he is a donor with tremendous wealth to give us. The guru is also in some way like a mirage of a lake in the desert. When we feel very thirsty in the desert we may think we see a lake or a brook, but really there is no brook or lake at all. In the same way, by holding out the fulfillment of our desires, the guru tantalizes us and inspires us to walk further into the desert of egolessness.

It seems that the important thing is the level of our own commitment—the extent to which we are willing to be embarrassed and humiliated through acknowledging our chaos, our confusion, our desire and grasping. We cannot work with these fixations if we do not acknowledge them and accept their existence. The more we accept them, the more we are able to let go of them. To that extent the guru is able to relate to us as the spokesman and ambassador of enlightenment.

The vajra master is like a master samurai instructing a novice. He trains us and encourages us to leap and take chances. He teaches us to cut through our hesitations. The appropriate way for us to relate to him is with simple, naked trust, without hope and fear. Our actual experiences of such trust may be momentary, but it is necessary at least to develop the right intellectual attitude toward trusting. Even though we may be unable to open completely, at least through understanding on the intellectual level we have the willingness to open, which is very important.

In fact, intellect plays a very important part in the process of opening. What we are referring to as *intellect* here is quite different from the ordinary notion of intellect as a faculty of philosophical speculation. Intellect in this case is clear seeing, real precision. Often when that precision arises fleetingly we try to sustain or recapture it, but it just fades away. It is necessary to work with that glimpse of precision, because it is what enables us to see the need for openness, but we must do so without trying to capture it. When such a glimpse of precision arises, we should disown it rather than trying to hang onto it or recreate it. Then at some point we start to develop confidence in ourselves; we develop confidence that such intellect is ours rather than a foreign element that we are introducing into our systems. It was not given to us from the outside, but was awakened within us. It will arise spontaneously, without being manipulated into place. That kind of awakening, that glimpse of intellectual understanding, is of great importance.

In many cases a glimpse of openness and precision brings unexpected fear. There may be a sense of being lost or exposed, a sense of vulnerability. That is simply a sign that ego is losing its grip on its territory; it is not a fundamental threat. The concept of threat only makes sense in relation to ego. If we have something to lose we feel threatened, and what we have to lose is our dear life, our ego. But if we have nothing to lose we cannot be threatened. The feeling of threat is a great stepping-stone, for it is the working basis for development. In fact, the student of tantra should be in a constant state of panic. Only then is his or her situation regarded as worthwhile. Such a state of panic serves two purposes: it overcomes the student's smugness and complacency, and it sharpens his clarity.

It has been said by the Tibetan master Pema Karpo and other great teachers that studying tantra is like riding on a razor. Finding we are on a razor's edge, we do not know whether we should try to slide down or try to freeze and stay put. If we only knew how to slide down a razor we might do it as easily as a child slides down a bannister. If we knew the nature of the blade we could do so. But if we do not know the nature of the blade and are just trying to prove ourselves, we might find ourselves sliced in half.

As I have said, warnings that alert the student to his actual situation are very important. The more warnings that are made about tantra, the more the student benefits. When the tantric master does not give enough warnings the student becomes a bad tantra student because he is not riding on the edge of a razor.

When students first hear about vajrayana, they may find it very fascinating. There are all kinds of exciting stories and possibilities, which become extremely seductive and appealing. Since the tantric approach is supposedly the quick path, students might think they should stop wasting time; they might feel they should get their money's worth and become enlightened as quickly as possible. Not only are they impatient but they are also cowardly: they do not want to have any pain or difficulties. Such students are not willing to open and expose themselves. They are not willing to face the successive panics that we are talking about. Actually, the panic is the source of openness, the source of questioning; it is the source of opening one's heart.

Usually when we panic we take a gasp of air, and that creates enormous freshness. That is what the tantric tradition is supposed to do. So if we are good tantric students we open ourselves each moment: we panic a thousand times a day, a hundred and eight times an hour. We are open constantly; we panic constantly. Thus the tantric approach to the world means refreshing our contact, reopening ourselves constantly so that we are able to perceive our cosmos properly and thoroughly. That sounds great, enormously promising, but there is a catch. Once we are in a position to be fascinated by the world, this naked world without a filter or screen, we too are naked. We are relating to the world without even any skin to protect our bodies. Experience becomes so intimate and so personal that it actually burns us or freezes us directly. We may become extremely sensitive and jumpy. It is possible that as we panic more, we may react more intensely. Experience becomes so direct and magical that it gives a direct shock. It is not like sitting back in a theater seat and being entertained by the fabulous world happening on the screen. It does not work that way. Instead it works mutually: to the extent that the naked world is uncovered, we too must be willing to expose ourselves.

Therefore tantra is very dangerous. It is electric. In addition to the naked electricity of ourselves and our world there is the vajra master, the teacher who introduces the possibilities of the true world to us. The teacher has the same electricity; the teacher is also naked. Traditionally he holds in his hand the symbol of a thunderbolt, which is called a *dorjé*, or *vajra*. With this vajra, if we and the cosmos are not connecting, the teacher can reignite the shock.

In this sense, the teacher has a lot of power, but not power *over* us in the manner of an egomaniac. As always, the teacher is a spokesperson of reality; he introduces us to our world. So the vajra master becomes extremely powerful and somewhat dangerous at this point. But he does not use this power simply to play tricks on us whenever he sees a weak point; he conducts his movements in a disciplined manner, according to the tradition. He touches us, he smells us, he looks at us, and he listens to our heartbeat. These processes are known as *abhishekas.*

Abhisheka is a Sanskrit word which literally means "anointment." We are bathed in holy water that is created by the master and the mandala around the master. Abhishekas are popularly known as "initiations," but that is actually a weak translation. The notion of abhisheka is different from a tribal initiation or rite of passage where we are accepted as a member of the tribe if we pass certain kinds of tests. It is entirely different. Our teacher's empowering us and our receiving the power depends both on our capability and the teacher's capability. The term *empowerment* is more appropriate than *initiation* because there is no tribe into which to be initiated. In other words, *abhisheka* does not mean being accepted into a closed circle; rather we are introduced into the universe. We cannot say the universe is a big tribe or that it is a big ego. It is just open space. The teacher empowers us so that we can enter our enlarged universe.

The teacher is the only embodiment of power in this transmission of energy. Without the teacher we cannot experience this properly, fully. And the only way to relate to such a teacher is through devotion. Devotion proceeds through various stages of unmasking until we reach the point of seeing the world directly and simply, without imposing our fabrications. This is called basic sanity. Devotion is a way of bringing us down to earth and of enabling us to develop this basic sanity through the challenges constantly presented by our relationship to our master.

We have to start out very simply. We have to give; we have to open up and display our ego; we have to present our ego as a gift to our spiritual friend. If we are unable to do that, then the path never begins because there is no working basis; there is nobody to walk on it.

PART TWO

Stages on the Path

5

Taking Refuge

"Becoming a refugee is acknowledging that we are groundless, and it is acknowledging that there is really no need for home, or ground. Taking refuge is an expression of freedom, because as refugees we are no longer bounded by the need for security. We are suspended in a no-man's land in which the only thing to do is to relate with the teachings and with ourselves."

Becoming a Refugee

In the Buddhist tradition, the purpose of taking refuge is to awaken from confusion and associate oneself with wakefulness. Taking refuge is a matter of commitment and acceptance and, at the same time, of openness and freedom. By taking the refuge vow we commit ourselves to freedom.

There is a general tendency to be involved in all kinds of fascinations and delusions, and nothing very much ever takes root in one's basic being. Everything in one's life experience, concerning spirituality or anything else, is purely a matter of shopping. Our lives consist of problems of pain, problems of pleasure, problems of points of view—problems about all kinds of alternatives—which make our existence complicated.

Taken from selected Refuge Vow ceremonies, 1973–1978.

We have allegiance to "that" and allegiance to "this." There are hundreds and millions of choices involved in our lives—particularly in regard to our sense of discipline, our ethics, and our spiritual path. People are very confused in this chaotic world about what is really the right thing to do. There are all kinds of rationales, taken from all kinds of traditions and philosophies. We may try to combine all of them together; sometimes they conflict, sometimes they work together harmoniously. But we are constantly shopping, and that is actually the basic problem.

It is not so much that there is something wrong with the traditions that exist around us; the difficulty is more our own personal conflict arising from wanting to have and to be the best. When we take refuge we give up some sense of seeing ourselves as the good citizen or as the hero of a success story. We might have to give up our past; we might have to give up our potential future. By taking this particular vow, we end our shopping in the spiritual supermarket. We decide to stick to a particular brand for the rest of our lives. We choose to stick to a particular staple diet and flourish on it.

When we take refuge we commit ourselves to the Buddhist path. This is not only a simple but also an extremely economical approach. Henceforth we will be on the particular path that was strategized, designed, and well thought-out twenty-five hundred years ago by the Buddha and the followers of his teaching. There is already a pattern and a tradition; there is already a discipline. We no longer have to run after that person or this person. We no longer have to compare our life-style with anybody else's. Once we take this step, we have no alternatives; there is no longer the entertainment of indulging in so-called freedom. We take a definite vow to enter a discipline of choicelessness—which saves us a lot of money, a lot of energy, and lots and lots of superfluous thinking.

Perhaps this approach may seem repressive, but it is really

based on a sympathetic attitude toward our situation. To work on ourselves is really only possible when there are no sidetracks, no exits. Usually we tend to look for solutions from something new, something outside: a change in society or politics, a new diet, a new theory. Or else we are always finding new things to blame our problems on, such as relationships, society, what have you. Working on oneself, without such exits or sidetracks, is the Buddhist path. We begin with the hinayana approach—the narrow path of simplicity and boredom.

By taking refuge, in some sense we become homeless refugees. Taking refuge does not mean saying that we are helpless and then handing all our problems over to somebody or something else. There will be no refugee rations, nor all kinds of security and dedicated help. The point of becoming a refugee is to give up our attachment to basic security. We have to give up our sense of home ground, which is illusory anyway. We might have a sense of home ground as where we were born and the way we look, but we don't actually have any home, fundamentally speaking. There is actually no solid basis of security in one's life. And because we don't have any home ground, we are lost souls, so to speak. Basically we are completely lost and confused and, in some sense, pathetic.

These are the particular problems that provide the reference point from which we build the sense of becoming a Buddhist. Relating to being lost and confused, we are more open. We begin to see that in seeking security we can't grasp onto anything; everything continually washes out and becomes shaky, constantly, all the time. And that is what is called life.

So becoming a refugee is acknowledging that we are homeless and groundless, and it is acknowledging that there is really no need for home, or ground. Taking refuge is an expression of freedom, because as refugees we are no longer bounded by the need for security. We are suspended in a no-man's land in which the only thing to do is to relate with the teachings and with ourselves.

The refuge ceremony represents a final decision. Acknowledging that the only real working basis is oneself and that there is no way around that, one takes refuge in the Buddha as an example, in the dharma as the path, and in the sangha as companionship. Nevertheless, it is a total commitment to oneself. The ceremony cuts the line that connects the ship to the anchor; it marks the beginning of an odyssey of loneliness. Still, it also includes the inspiration of the preceptor—in this case myself—and his lineage. The participation of the preceptor is a kind of guarantee that you will not be getting back into the question of security as such, that you will continue to acknowledge your aloneness and work on yourself without leaning on anyone. Finally you become a real person, standing on your own feet. At that point, everything starts with you.

This particular journey is like that of the first settlers. We have come to no-man's land and have not been provided with anything at all. Here we are, and we have to make everything with our own bare hands. We are, in our own way, pioneers: each is a historical person on his own journey. It is an individual pioneership of building spiritual ground. Everything has to be made and produced by us. Nobody is going to throw us little chocolate chips or console us with goodies. So we have to learn how to milk the cows. In fact, we have to find the cows first—they might be wild animals at this point—and we have to tame them, put them into a corral, milk them, and nurse their young. We have to learn how to make a sword: we have to melt the stone and make iron out of it. We have to make everything. We came here barefoot and naked, and we even have to make our own clothes—our own shoes and hats, whatever we need. This is the starting point, right here at this point. It is necessary to make this beginning.

If we adopt a prefabricated religion that tells us exactly the best way to do everything, it is as though that religion provides a complete home with wall-to-wall carpeting. We get completely spoiled. We don't have to put out any effort or energy, so our dedication and devotion have no fiber. We wind up complaining because we didn't get the deluxe toilet tissue that we used to get. So at this point, rather than walking into a nicely prepared hotel or luxurious house, we are starting from the primitive level. We have to figure out how we are going to build our city and how we are going to relate with our comrades who are doing the same thing.

We have to work with the sense of sacredness and richness and the magical aspect of our experience. And this has to be done on the level of our everyday existence, which is a personal level, an extremely personal level. There are no scapegoats. When you take refuge you become responsible to yourself as a follower of the dharma. You are isolating yourself from the rest of your world in the sense that the world is not going to help you any more; it is no longer regarded as a source of salvation. It is just a mirage, *maya*. It might mock you, play music for you, and dance for you, but nevertheless the path and the inspiration of the path are up to *you*. You have to do it. And the meaning of taking refuge is that you are *going* to do it. You commit yourself as a refugee to yourself, no longer thinking that some divine principle that exists in the holy law or holy scriptures is going to save you. It is very personal. You experience a sense of loneliness, aloneness—a sense that there is no savior, no help. But at the same time there is a sense of belonging: you belong to a tradition of loneliness where people work together.

You might say: "I have been this way for a long time. Why does there have to be a ceremony?" The ceremony is important because then there will be a particular time and a date on which your commitment takes place. There will be one particular fraction of a second after which you are committed to yourself, and you will know that very precisely and clearly. It is the same as celebrating the New Year: when the clock strikes twelve, we finally say "Happy New Year." There is that particular moment. So we make sure that there are no fuzzy edges to your memory or commitment. You are a slippery fish, and you have to be provided with some kind of net. The net is the situation of taking refuge that you are caught in; and the fisherman, the person who fishes you out of the water, is the preceptor. At that point the fish has no choice but to surrender to the fisherman. Without the ceremony, somehow it doesn't work; the whole thing is left too much to your imagination and your slippery subjectifying process.

When you become a refugee, a follower of the Buddha's teaching, you get onto a train that is without reverse and without brakes. The train comes along and pulls up to a certain station at a certain time. You get onto the train, then the whistle toots and off you go.

So the refuge ceremony is a landmark of becoming a Buddhist, a nontheist. You no longer have to make sacrifices in somebody's else's name, trying to get yourself saved or to earn redemption. You no longer have to push yourself overboard so that you will be smiled at by that guy who watches us, the old man with the beard. As far as Buddhists are concerned, the sky is blue and the grass is green—in the summer, of course. As far as Buddhists are concerned, human beings are very important and they have never been condemned—except by their own confusion, which is understandable. If nobody shows you a path, any kind of path, you're going to be confused. That is not your fault. But now you are being shown the path and you are beginning to work with a particular teacher. And at this point nobody is confused. You are what you are, the teachings are what they are, and I am what I am—a preceptor to ordain you as Buddhist persons.

This is a very joyous situation as far as I am concerned: we are going to work together from the beginning to the end.

Taking refuge in the Buddha as an example, taking refuge in the dharma as the path, and taking refuge in the sangha as companionship is very clean-cut, very definite, very precise, and very clear. People have done this for the past twenty-five hundred years of the Buddhist tradition. By taking refuge you receive that particular heritage into your own system; you join that particular wisdom that has existed for twenty-five hundred years without interruption and without corruption. It is very direct and very simple.

Taking Refuge in the Buddha

You take refuge in the Buddha not as a savior—not with the feeling that you have found something to make you secure—but as an example, as someone you can emulate. He is an example of an ordinary human being who saw through the deceptions of life, both on the ordinary and spiritual levels. The Buddha found the awakened state of mind by relating with the situations that existed around him: the confusion, chaos, and insanity. He was able to look at those situations very clearly and precisely. He disciplined himself by working on his own mind, which was the source of all the chaos and confusion. Instead of becoming an anarchist and blaming society, he worked on himself and he attained what is known as *bodhi,* or enlightenment. The final and ultimate breakthrough took place, and he was able to teach and work with sentient beings without any inhibition.

The example of the Buddha's life is applicable because he started out in basically the same kind of life that we lead, with the same confusion. But he renounced that life in order to find the truth. He went through a lot of religious "trips." He tried to work with the theistic world of the Hinduism of the time, and he realized there were a lot of problems with that. Then, instead of looking for an outside solution, he began working on himself. He began pulling up his own socks, so to speak, and he became a buddha. Until he did that, he was just a wishy-washy spiritual tripper. So taking refuge in the Buddha as an example is realizing that our case history is in fact completely comparable with his, and then deciding that we are going to follow his example and do what he did.

By taking refuge you begin to realize that you can actually compete with the Buddha. You can do that. Twenty-five hundred years ago one person, who also had to deal with his daily living situation, managed to awaken himself and experience the pain of life. He was able to work through that and work along with it and finally attain buddhahood, enlightenment. That person was called Gautama, the chief of the Shakya tribe. He was a prince who had all kinds of luxury and security and who felt alienated from his basic state of sanity. So he decided to question the whole thing. He escaped from his kingdom, and he practiced meditation in the jungles and the woods. The only friends or spiritual teachers he could find were all spiritual materialists: they were using meditation to fortify ego. He tried all kinds of physical gimmicks—holding his breath, turning upside down, sitting in the middle of a campfire—and he found them all futile. Then he began to arouse himself, to make his own liberation by himself. So he won enlightenment single-handedly. He was such a smart person that he was able to get out of the psychological materialism of trying to shore up ego through ideas, and out of spiritual materialism as well. He was able to win a victory over both kinds of materialism. Henceforth he was known as the Buddha, the Awakened One.

We can do that as well. Thousands of people in the Buddha's tradition have done so. We have psychological materialism and spiritual materialism happening constantly in our lives, so we have the same material to work on. There is no doubt that we have plenty of that kind of food for our minds.

One of the big steps in the Buddha's development was his realization that there is no reason we should believe in or expect anything greater than the basic inspiration that exists in us already. This is a nontheistic tradition: the Buddha gave up relying on any kind of divine principle that would descend on him and solve his problems. So taking refuge in the Buddha in no way means regarding him as a god. He was simply a person who practiced, worked, studied, and experienced things personally. With that in mind, taking refuge in the Buddha amounts to renouncing misconceptions about divine existence. Since we possess what is known as *buddha-nature,* enlightened intelligence, we don't have to borrow somebody else's glory. We are not all that helpless. We have our own resources already. A hierarchy of divine principles is irrelevant. It is very much up to us. Our individuality has produced our own world. The whole situation is very personal.

Taking Refuge in the Dharma

Then we take refuge in the *teachings* of the Buddha, the dharma. We take refuge in the dharma as path. In this way we find that everything in our life situation is a constant process of learning and discovery. We do not regard some things as secular and some things as sacred, but everything is regarded as *truth*—which is the definition of dharma. Dharma is also *passionlessness,* which in this case means not grasping, holding on, or trying to possess—it means non-aggression.

Usually, the basic thread that runs through our experience

is our desire to have a purely goal-oriented process: everything, we feel, should be done in relation to our ambition, our competitiveness, our one-upmanship. That is what usually drives us to become greater professors, greater mechanics, greater carpenters, greater poets. Dharma—passionlessness—cuts through this small, goal-oriented vision, so that everything becomes purely a learning process. This permits us to relate with our lives fully and properly. So, taking refuge in the dharma as path, we develop the sense that it is worthwhile to walk on this earth. Nothing is regarded as just a waste of time; nothing is seen as a punishment or as a cause of resentment and complaint.

This aspect of taking refuge is particularly applicable in America, where it is quite fashionable to blame everything on others and to feel that all kinds of elements in one's relationships or surroundings are unhealthy or polluted. We react with resentment. But once we begin to do that, there is no way. The world becomes divided into two sections: sacred and profane, or that which is good and proper and that which is regarded as a bad job or a necessary evil. Taking refuge in the dharma, taking a passionless approach, means that all of life is regarded as a fertile situation and a learning situation, always. Whatever occurs—pain or pleasure, good or bad, justice or injustice—is part of the learning process. So there is nothing to blame; everything is the path, everything is dharma.

That passionless quality of dharma is an expression of *nirvana*—freedom, or openness. And once we have that approach, then any spiritual practice we might go through becomes a part of the learning situation, rather than merely ritualistic or spiritual, or a matter of religious obligation. The whole process becomes integral and natural.

We have always tried to make sense out of the looseness and unsatisfactoriness of life by trying to make things secure and trying to freeze that washed-out quality into some definite story line. But now we can no longer make very much sense out of it. Things constantly change, constantly move, constantly become something else. So now we begin to work with the basic premise that that flow, or fluctuation of ups and downs, in our lives can be seen as a mirror reflection, or as waves in the ocean. Things come close to us and we can almost hold onto them, but then they disappear. Things seem as if they are just about to make sense; then suddenly there is immense confusion and what was about to make sense seems quite remote, a million miles away. We are constantly trying to grasp something, and we lose it just as we think we have our fingertips on it. This is the source of frustration, suffering—or *duhkha,* as the Buddha called it. Duhkha is the First Noble Truth. Recognizing that, we begin to make sense out of nothing, so to speak. Transitoriness begins to become more meaningful than trying to freeze truth into a solid lump. That realization—understanding the fluctuation that goes on and working with it—is the meaning of taking refuge in the dharma.

This approach involves a quality of directness and absence of deception—or we might even say absence of politeness. It means that we actually face the facts of life directly, personally. We do not have to come up with any padding of politeness or ordinary cheapness, but we actually experience life. And it is very ordinary life: pain is pain and pleasure is pleasure. We don't have to use another word or innuendo. Pain and pleasure and confusion—everything takes place very nakedly. We are simply ordinary. But nakedness and absence of politeness don't necessarily mean being completely savage. We are naked just in going without the padding that we usually provide ourselves with. With our friends, with our relatives, in everything that goes on, we can afford to be very simple and direct and personal.

In that way all the things that go on in life—economic, domestic, and spiritual—are no longer regarded as belonging in separate compartments, but everything is combined into one situation. That is what it means to follow the path of the dharma. Neither hot, intense moments of complete claustrophobia nor cool, noncaring moments are regarded as either extraordinarily good or extraordinarily terrible. Those are just the fashions of life that we are involved in. It is a natural process taking place constantly. Taking refuge in the dharma means relating to everything that happens, from the splinter in your little finger to your granddad's committing suicide in your name, from the littlest to the biggest, as part of that natural process. There are all sorts of shapes of journeys taking place constantly. And all of them are just a trick; they are just interesting facets of life.

But still you can't just say, "Let's leave it alone. Let's just watch everything and become great poets." Oh no. You can't just write poems about it, play music about it, or dance to it. You have to get into all those facets of life completely. And getting into them is the meaning of *path*—they become the path. That is accompanied by the practice of meditation, which actually makes the whole thing very clear and precise. The clearer our minds become, the more real and vivid become all the little things that are promising and threatening: the hopes and fears, the pains and pleasures.

The dharma is traditionally divided into two aspects. The first is *what has been told,* which means the holy scriptures, the books of the teachings which have been written from the time of the Buddha until the present. Those sacred books, which have been handed down from generation to generation, contain the truth of *what has been experienced,* which is the second aspect of the dharma. Throughout the Buddhist lineage, individuals have experienced reality and truth within the teachings, and this can also be experienced by you. It is a discovery within your own life that happens both with your teacher and by yourself. It happens particularly through your experience of meditation, both in formal sitting practice and in meditation-in-action.

Taking refuge in the dharma means that the experiences that go through your life, pain and pleasure alike, are also sacred teachings. The teachings are not sacred because they were discovered in space or because they came from the sky and were given by divine principles. But the teachings were discovered in the heart, in human hearts—in buddha-nature. For example the Buddhist canon, the *Tripitaka,* is based on *somebody's* experience. It is all *somebody's* discourse. The one hundred and eight volumes of sutras are spoken words— communications from one human being to another. The Buddha, who was fully awakened, was communicating with other human beings who were not awakened, were half-awakened, or were in a somewhat-awakened state. The truth has never come from the sky; it has always come from the human condition. The Four Noble Truths of the Buddha describe the human experience of pain, the origin of pain, the possibilities of salvation, and the possibilities of the path. These are very literal truths; they are the direct truth, rather than something that was manufactured upstairs.

So in taking refuge in the dharma, the books of the teachings are not regarded as mystical writings that were created by the clouds and the sun meeting together and engraving script on a tablet. These books were written with ink and pen on pieces of paper. The memories of the seminars, talks, and discourses that Lord Buddha gave were recorded simply as a description of what an awakened man said, how an awakened person conducted himself in the living situation. So taking refuge in the dharma has nothing to do with unearthly influence; it has nothing to do with Martians, and it has nothing to do with Jehovah either—but it definitely has something to do with sanity. Taking refuge in the dharma means that human beings' experience can be heightened so much that, extraordinarily, we can actually awaken ourselves within ourselves.

Once again, whatever goes on in our minds is a learning situation: the love and hate relationships that evolve around us, the sense of misfortune, the sense of being lucky, the sense of defeat, the sense of arrogance and egohood, the sense of patriotism, the sense of smartness, the sense of being special, and the sense of confusion—all are included in our particular basic situation. That *is* the path. It is the only way; it is the only thing that we can work on. We cannot just milk the cow of the guru all the time, whenever we are hungry or thirsty. But we can experience our life-style and our process of development according to the dharma of what has been told. Then we become in tune with the dharma of what has been experienced at the same time, as the followers of the dharma have done in the past—which is very powerful and very meaningful for all of us.

Taking Refuge in the Sangha

Having taken refuge in the Buddha as an example and the dharma as path, then we take refuge in the sangha as companionship. That means that we have a lot of friends, fellow refugees, who are also confused, and who are working with the same guidelines as we are. Everybody is simultaneously struggling with their own discipline. As the members of the sangha experience a sense of dignity, and their sense of taking refuge in the Buddha, dharma, and sangha begins to evolve, they are able to act as a reminder and to provide feedback for each other. Your friends in the sangha provide a continual reference point which creates a continual learning process. They act as mirror reflections to remind you or warn you in living situations. That is the kind of companionship that is meant by *sangha.* We are all in the same boat; we share a sense of trust and a sense of larger-scale, organic friendship.

At the same time, you have to stand on your own two feet. A sense of individuality and a sense of comradeship are both involved. You are working together and helping each other, but you are not helping so much that you become addicted to each other's help. If you lean on somebody in a weak moment of your life, the person you lean on may seem strong, but he will also begin to catch your weakness. If he falls down, you will fall down too. If the principle were just to lean on one another, we could have thousands of people all leaning on each other, but then if one person fell down, everybody would fall down. The whole thing would collapse, like an old dilapidated building, and there would be great chaos. It would be a suicidal process, with thousands all collapsing at the same time—which would be very messy, very dusty.

So taking refuge in the sangha means being willing to work with your fellow students—your brothers and sisters in the dharma—while being independent at the same time. That's a very important point here, actually, in terms of taking the refuge vow. Nobody imposes his or her heavy notions on the rest of the sangha. If one particular person tries to act as a catalyst or spokesman for the whole sangha, that is regarded as frivolous. If someone is extremely timid, credulous, and dependent, that is also regarded as frivolous. Instead, each member of the sangha is an individual who is on the path in a different way from all the others. It is because of that that you get constant feedback of all kinds: negative and positive, encouraging and discouraging. These very rich resources become available to you when you take refuge in the sangha, the fellowship of students. It is as though yeast is put into a batch of hundreds of grains of barley. Each grain begins to fill up with yeast, until finally there is a huge, beautiful, gigantic vat of beer. Everything is yeasted completely; each one of the grains has become powerful individually—so the whole thing becomes a real world.

The sangha is the community of people who have the perfect right to cut through your trips and feed you with their wisdom, as well as the perfect right to demonstrate their own neurosis and be seen through by you. The companionship within the sangha is a kind of clean friendship—without expectation, without demand, but at the same time, fulfilling.

The sangha are a source of learning as much as the spiritual friend or teacher. So there is a need for some trust in the sangha. But we have to make a very definite point here: we are speaking of the *organized* sangha, which is the sangha of practitioners who actually sit together, practice together, and also work on themselves. Without that sangha, we have no reference point; we are thrown back into the big samsaric soup, and we have no idea who or what we are. We are lost.

So we no longer regard ourselves as lone wolves who have such a good thing going on the side that we don't have to relate with anybody at all, whether the organization, the sitting practice, or the sangha at large. At the same time we must not simply go along with the crowd. Either extreme is too secure. The idea is one of constantly opening, giving up completely. There is a lot of need for giving up.

Joining the particular club of lonely people who call themselves the sangha is a very heroic thing to do. Conventionally, you don't join anything unless all the ground is secured. Normally you pay a certain amount of money to join a particular club, and that gives you the kind of service that makes you feel good and secure. But at this point it is a very impersonal approach; in a strange way it is also very personal. You are willing to work with your loneliness in a group. The sangha is made up of thousands of people who are alone together, working together with their own loneliness, their own aloneness. Together they make an orchestra; you are able to dance with its music, and that is a very personal experience. You begin to join that particular energy, which allows individuality and spontaneity as well as non-aggression.

The sense of trust and frankness in the sangha frightens a lot of people; nevertheless, genuine communication takes place. Also, the level of sophistication of the sangha naturally becomes heightened. We cannot regard the sangha as an in-group situation, like a cheap, greasy spoon household of brown-rice eaters. At this level the sangha is an immaculate household, with immaculate relationships, in which experiences with each other occur personally. The real sangha is made up of dedicated people who are actually working on themselves. They haven't developed any fantastic tricks, magic, extraordinary philosophy, or anything like that. From that point of view, such companionship might seem somewhat boring, too ordinary. Nevertheless, it is very real. Quite possibly, you might occasionally seek out extraordinary friends and pursuits, but somehow those pursuits turn out to be purely plastic, part of a dream world, so that you return to the real sangha, the real people who actually care about themselves, care about you as a friend, and relate with the whole situation completely, without any areas shielded through a consensus of weakness.

Having taken the refuge vow, there are three types of change that take place: change of attitude, change of mark, and change of name.

Change of Attitude

Change of attitude involves developing a sense of sympathy toward oneself, and therefore toward the world. One's attitude changes to that of nonaggression and passionlessness. Aggression refers to a general sense of uptightness and unfriendliness—of regarding the world as an object to do battle with. And in passion, one is trying to win something over, engaging in continual one-upmanship. In either case one has a constant battle going on with the world—that is to say, with oneself.

When you change your attitude you develop an awareness that allows you to be friendly with yourself and thus with the rest of sentient beings. There is some sense of gentleness. This is connected with commitment to the practice of meditation, which creates an openness to your own ups and downs, and a willingness to go along with them and work on them. You develop such a thorough relationship with the teachings that they become part of you. The Three Jewels—the Buddha, the dharma, and the sangha—become a part of your existence and you thrive on that, you work with that, you live on that. You do not become a religious person as such, but you become gentle, soft, and very amiable and workable. You don't create defense mechanisms all the time.

As a Buddhist, you are less greedy. If your breakfast isn't cooked just the way you want it, you give in and eat the crummy breakfast you don't like. There is a sense that you can give an inch in your demands—just a little inch, a fraction of a second. So trying to give in, which is the change of attitude, is very important. Usually we don't want to give in: "I want to have my own way. I want complete, one hundred percent hospitality; and if I don't get it, I'm going to fight for my rights," and so forth. This is problematic and anti-Buddhist in some sense.

Another aspect of the change of attitude is that when you become a full-fledged Buddhist you feel that your life is workable in any situation. You don't feel alienated from your problems, and you don't try to put yourself in some kind of special spiritual orbit. You can be very gentle and friendly to yourself and other people and relate with the world—which seems to be the basic point of the Buddhist teachings. But you don't have to conduct yourself with the superficial smile and gleaming, honey-smeared attitude of "love and light." This is a genuine experience: you enter the tradition of the nonaggressive state of mind, and you are capable of conducting yourself in that way without artifice.

Nonaggression in this context also means refraining from taking life; you refrain from the personal rejection of animals, enemies, human beings, or whatever. People sometimes take pride in killing flies; in that kind of little situation they become involved in some kind of "gotcha!" mentality. That's a very savage kind of behavior. Becoming a follower of the dharma means becoming more sophisticated in the fundamental sense. You begin to pay attention to the details of your daily life situation, which become more important, and in fact sacred.

Such an attitude cannot be made up. It only comes from lots of meditation practice; that seems to be the only way. The sitting practice of meditation seems to produce gentleness and compassion naturally.

Change of Mark

Change of mark is closely related to change of attitude. Once you begin to behave with nonaggression, you begin to show signs of the sanity that is already in you. You don't actually have to try to prove anything to your relatives, your parents, your friends. The words don't count; the people around you can simply and actually appreciate the development of gentleness and reasonableness taking place in you. It is not that you are trying to be polite and understanding in the cheap sense, but you are trying to be polite and understanding beyond consideration of your own personal comfort. So some sense of gentleness and sympathy takes place, and that is the mark of being Buddhist. You begin to turn into a different breed of man. You become a gentle, considerate person who is open and brave at the same time.

You are not suddenly going to become a glowing, happy, easy-going, enlightened person, obviously. But the whole idea is that it is possible, if one's sitting practice and discipline are taking place, that one's personality could change from that painful, serious, deep-down level of neurosis into something open, sharp, profound, and delightful. This is not particularly a salesman's pitch—that change has been happening to students throughout the whole of our experience in this country.

Change of Name

Traditionally, in Tibet and other Buddhist countries, the parents would give their child a nickname that was used during childhood. Then, when the child took the refuge vow, they would be given a Buddhist name. The nickname would be phased out, or maybe just used occasionally among one's close circle of relatives, and the Buddhist name would then be assumed. In this setting, that situation may be somewhat sticky, so I like to leave it up to each person whether or not they want to use their refuge name. The point is that when you are called by your Buddhist name, you should assume that particular attitude of gentleness. Your name should act as a reminder rather than as something that provides further identification for your ego or that is just purely a handle.

The meaning behind the name is connected with some kind of inspiration that you might develop. It is not necessarily a flattering name, nor is it condescending—but it is some kind of message. Your Buddhist name represents an encouragement for some kind of development in your personality which is connected with the practice of meditation—some sense of your individual style in approaching the dharma.

The Refuge Vow Ceremony

The main part of the refuge vow ceremony involves offering three prostrations then repeating the refuge formula three times: "I take refuge in the Buddha, I take refuge in the dharma, I take refuge in the sangha." I should explain the purpose of prostrations. There are all kinds of self-made spiritual journeys that we might be able to take, but what is important and necessary is to surrender our ego trips. Such surrender makes us much more self-made and much more closely and personally related with reality. So the idea of the prostrations is to surrender your personal clingings of all kinds so that you can begin to tune in to this particular path.

When you prostrate you hold your palms together successively at the level of your forehead, your throat, and your heart, which represents surrendering your body, speech, and mind to the Buddha, dharma, and sangha without expecting anything in return. Prostrating on the ground is very significant; it means surrendering finally. You are making a *real* commitment; you are willing to give in completely to the choiceless sanity of the earth and become a refugee in no-man's land. The past, present, and future lineage holders are represented by this earth. You may get pissed off at this earth; you may feel very good about this earth; you may feel very unconcerned about this earth—but still the earth remains here, and it remains solid. Bowing yourself down on this earth is surrendering yourself to this basic sanity.

You do the three prostrations to the shrine, which represents our heritage. More explicitly, it represents the lineage of those who transmit awakened mind, which exists in the past, present, and future. You are also prostrating to the preceptor, who is the inheritor of this lineage. The method used in the past is no longer a myth, but is real and living. You have a living Buddhist in front of you.

Kneeling and repeating the refuge formula three times is the actual refuge-taking. It has three aspects: acknowledging oneself, acknowledging one's need for protection, and acknowledging the other. When you say, "*I* take refuge," you are requesting to be accepted as a refugee. And when you say, "in the Buddha, dharma, sangha," you are acknowledging the other, which is the example, the path, and the sense of community. In this situation you have to be very deliberate, precisely aware of all the processes you are going through.

You repeat the refuge formula three times. The first time is preparing the ground; the second time you are going further; and the third time you have actually gone completely.

The discipline of taking refuge is something more than a doctrinal or ritual thing: you are being physically infected with commitment to the buddhadharma; Buddhism is transmitted into your system. Something in the lineage which is very physical, almost at the level of chemistry, enters your heart as your commitment to openness takes place. The third time you say "I take refuge in the sangha," the preceptor snaps his fingers. That is the moment of real transmission. At that moment the sperm, so to speak, enters your system and you become part of the lineage. From that moment onward, you are a follower of the practicing lineage of the Kagyü. At that particular point, the energy, the power, and the blessing of basic sanity that has existed in the lineage for twenty-five hundred years, in an unbroken tradition and discipline from the time of Buddha, enters your system, and you finally become a full-fledged follower of buddha-dharma. You are a living future buddha at that point.

6

The Bodhisattva Vow

"Taking the bodhisattva vow has tremendous power for the very reason that it is not something we do just for the pleasure of ego. It is beyond oneself. Taking the vow is like planting the seed of a fast-growing tree, whereas something done for the benefit of ego is like sowing a grain of sand. Planting such a seed as the bodhisattva vow undermines ego and leads to a tremendous expansion of perspective. Such heroism, or bigness of mind, fills all of space completely, utterly, absolutely."

The bodhisattva vow is the commitment to put others before oneself. It is a statement of willingness to give up one's own well-being, even one's own enlightenment, for the sake of others. And a bodhisattva is simply a person who lives in the spirit of that vow, perfecting the qualities known as the six *paramitas*—generosity, discipline, patience, exertion, meditation, and transcendental knowledge—in his effort to liberate beings.

Taking the bodhisattva vow implies that instead of holding onto our individual territory and defending it tooth and nail we become open to the world that we are living in. It means we are willing to take on greater responsibility, im-

Taken from selected Bodhisattva Vow ceremonies, 1973–1978.

mense responsibility. In fact it means taking a big chance. But taking such a chance is not false heroism or personal eccentricity. It is a chance that has been taken in the past by millions of bodhisattvas, enlightened ones, and great teachers. So a tradition of responsibility and openness has been handed down from generation to generation; and now we too are participating in the sanity and dignity of this tradition.

There is an unbroken lineage of bodhisattvas, springing from the great bodhisattvas Avalokiteshvara, Vajrapani, and Manjushri. It is unbroken because no one in that lineage, through generations and centuries, has indulged himself in self-preservation. Instead these bodhisattvas have constantly tried to work for the benefit of all sentient beings. This heritage of friendship has continued unbroken up to the present day, not as a myth but as a living inspiration.

The sanity of this tradition is very powerful. What we are doing in taking the bodhisattva vow is magnificent and glorious. It is such a wholehearted and full tradition that those who have not joined it might feel somewhat wretched by comparison. They might be envious of such richness. But joining this tradition also makes tremendous demands on us. We no longer are intent on creating comfort for ourselves; we work with others. This implies working with *our* other as well as the *other* other. *Our* other is our projections and our sense of privacy and longing to make things comfortable for ourselves. The *other* other is the phenomenal world outside, which is filled with screaming kids, dirty dishes, confused spiritual practitioners, and assorted sentient beings.

So taking the bodhisattva vow is a real commitment based on the realization of the suffering and confusion of oneself and others. The only way to break the chain reaction of confusion and pain and to work our way outward into the awakened state of mind is to take responsibility ourselves. If we do not deal with this situation of confusion, if we do not do something about it ourselves, nothing will ever happen. We cannot count on others to do it for us. It is our responsibility, and we have the tremendous power to change the course of the world's karma. So in taking the bodhisattva vow, we are acknowledging that we are not going to be instigators of further chaos and misery in the world, but we are going to be liberators, bodhisattvas, inspired to work on ourselves as well as with other people.

There is tremendous inspiration in having decided to work with others. We no longer try to build up our own grandiosity. We simply try to become human beings who are genuinely able to help others; that is, we develop precisely that quality of selflessness which is generally lacking in our world. Following the example of Gautama Buddha, who gave up his kingdom to dedicate his time to working with sentient beings, we are finally becoming useful to society.

We each might have discovered some little truth (such as the truth about poetry or the truth about photography or the truth about amoebas) which can be of help to others. But we tend to use such a truth simply to build up our own credentials. Working with our little truths, little by little, is a cowardly approach. In contrast, the work of a bodhisattva is without credentials. We could be beaten, kicked, or just unappreciated, but we remain kind and willing to work with others. It is a totally noncredit situation. It is truly genuine and very powerful.

Taking this mahayana approach of benevolence means giving up privacy and developing a sense of greater vision. Rather than focusing on our own little projects, we expand our vision immensely to embrace working with the rest of the world, the rest of the galaxies, the rest of the universes.

Putting such a broad vision into practice requires that we relate to situations very clearly and perfectly. In order to drop our self-centeredness, which both limits our view and clouds our actions, it is necessary for us to develop a sense of compassion. Traditionally this is done by first developing compassion toward oneself, then toward someone very close to us, and finally toward all sentient beings, including our enemies. Ultimately we regard all sentient beings with as much emotional involvement as if they were our own mothers. We may not require such a traditional approach at this point, but we can develop some sense of ongoing openness and gentleness. The point is that somebody has to make the first move.

Usually we are in a stalemate with our world: "Is he going to say he is sorry to me first, or am I going to apologize to him first?" But in becoming a bodhisattva we break that barrier: we do not wait for the other person to make the first move; we have decided to do it ourselves. People have a lot of problems and they suffer a great deal, obviously. And we have only half a grain of sand's worth of awareness of the suffering happening in this country alone, let alone in the rest of the world. Millions of people in the world are suffering because of their lack of generosity, discipline, patience, exertion, meditation, and transcendental knowledge. The point of making the first move by taking the bodhisattva vow is not to convert people to our particular view, necessarily; the idea is that we should contribute something to the world simply by our own way of relating, by our own gentleness.

In taking the bodhisattva vow, we acknowledge that the world around us is workable. From the bodhisattva's point of view it is not a hard-core, incorrigible world. It can be worked with within the inspiration of the buddhadharma, following the example of Lord Buddha and the great bodhisattvas. We can join their campaign to work with sentient beings properly, fully, and thoroughly—without grasping, without confusion, and without aggression. Such a campaign is a natural development of the practice of meditation because meditation brings a growing sense of egolessness.

By taking the bodhisattva vow, we open ourselves to many demands. If we are asked for help, we should not refuse; if we are invited to be someone's guest, we should not refuse; if we are invited to be a parent, we should not refuse. In other words, we have to have some kind of interest in taking care of people, some appreciation of the phenomenal world and its occupants. It is not an easy matter. It requires that we not be completely tired and put off by people's heavy-handed neurosis, ego-dirt, ego-puke, or ego-diarrhea; instead we are appreciative and willing to clean up for them. It is a sense of softness whereby we allow situations to take place in spite of little inconveniences; we allow situations to bother us, to overcrowd us.

Taking the bodhisattva vow means that we are inspired to put the teachings of Buddhism into practice in our everyday lives. In doing so we are mature enough not to hold anything back. Our talents are not rejected but are utilized as part of the learning process, part of the practice. A bodhisattva may teach the dharma in the form of intellectual understanding, artistic understanding, or even business understanding. So in committing ourselves to the bodhisattva path, we are resuming our talents in an enlightened way, not being threatened or confused by them. Earlier our talents may have been "trips," part of the texture of our confusion, but now we are bringing them back to life. Now they can blossom with the help of the teaching, the teacher, and our practice. This does not mean that we completely perfect our whole situation on the spot. There will still be confusion taking place, of course! But at the same time there is also a glimpse of openness and unlimited potentiality.

It is necessary at this point to take a leap in terms of trusting ourselves. We can actually correct any aggression or lack of compassion—anything antibodhisattvalike—as it happens; we can recognize our own neurosis and work with it rather than trying to cover it up or throw it out. In this way one's neurotic thought pattern, or "trip," slowly dissolves. Whenever we work with our neurosis in such a direct way, it becomes compassionate action.

The usual human instinct is to feed ourselves first and only make friends with others if they can feed us. This could be called "ape instinct." But in the case of the bodhisattva vow, we are talking about a kind of superhuman instinct which is much deeper and more full than that. Inspired by this instinct, we are willing to feel empty and deprived and confused. But something comes out of our willingness to feel that way, which is that we can help somebody else at the same time. So there is room for our confusion and chaos and egocenteredness: they become stepping-stones. Even the irritations that occur in the practice of the bodhisattva path become a way of confirming our commitment.

By taking the bodhisattva vow, we actually present ourselves as the property of sentient beings: depending on the situation, we are willing to be a highway, a boat, a floor, or a house. We allow other sentient beings to use us in whatever way they choose. As the earth sustains the atmosphere and outer space accommodates the stars, galaxies, and all the rest, we are willing to carry the burdens of the world. We are inspired by the physical example of the universe. We offer ourselves as wind, fire, air, earth, and water—all the elements.

But it is necessary and very important to avoid *idiot compassion*. If one handles fire wrongly, he gets burned; if one rides a horse badly, he gets thrown. There is a sense of earthy reality. Working with the world requires some kind of practical intelligence. We cannot just be "love-and-light" bodhisattvas. If we do not work intelligently with sentient beings, quite possibly our help will become addictive rather than beneficial. People will become addicted to our help in the same way they become addicted to sleeping pills. By trying to get more and more help they will become weaker and weaker. So for the benefit of sentient beings, we need to open ourselves with an attitude of fearlessness. Because of people's natural tendency toward indulgence, sometimes it is best for us to be direct and cutting. The bodhisattva's approach is to help others to help themselves. It is analogous to the elements: earth, water, air, and fire always reject us when we try to use them in a manner that is beyond what is suitable, but at the same time, they offer themselves generously to be worked with and used properly.

One of the obstacles to bodhisattva discipline is an absence of humor; we could take the whole thing too seriously. Approaching the benevolence of a bodhisattva in a militant fashion doesn't quite work. Beginners are often overly concerned with their own practice and their own development, approaching mahayana in a very hinayana style. But that serious militancy is quite different from the lightheartedness and joy of the bodhisattva path. In the beginning you may have to fake being open and joyous. But you should at least attempt to be open, cheerful, and, at the same time, brave. This requires that you continuously take some sort of leap. You may leap like a flea, a grasshopper, a frog, or finally, like a bird, but some sort of leap is always taking place on the bodhisattva path.

There is a tremendous sense of celebration and joy in finally being able to join the family of the buddhas. At last we have decided to claim our inheritance, which is enlightenment. From the perspective of doubt, whatever enlightened quality exists in us may seem small-scale. But from the perspective of actuality, a fully developed enlightened being exists in us already. Enlightenment is no longer a myth: it does exist, it is workable, and we are associated with it thoroughly and fully. So we have no doubts as to whether we are on the path or not. It is obvious that we have made a commitment and that we are going to develop this ambitious project of becoming a buddha. Taking the bodhisattva vow is an expression of settling down and making ourselves at home in this world. We are not concerned that somebody is going to attack us or destroy us. We are constantly exposing ourselves for the benefit of sentient beings. In fact, we are even giving up our ambition to attain enlightenment in favor of relieving the suffering and difficulties of people. Nevertheless, helplessly, we attain enlightenment anyway. Bodhisattvas and great tathagatas in the past have taken this step, and we too can do so. It is simply up to us whether we are going to accept this richness or reject it and settle for a poverty-stricken mentality.

Transplanting Bodhichitta

The bodhisattva vow is a leap in which we begin to let go of our egocentric approach to spiritual development. In the absolute sense, the bodhisattva vow is the complete transplantation of *bodhichitta,* awakened mind, into our hearts—a complete binding of ourselves with the gentleness and compassion of our inherent wakefulness. But we do not become complete bodhisattvas at once; we simply put ourselves forward as candidates for bodhisattvahood. Because of this we speak of relative and absolute bodhichitta. Relative bodhichitta is like having the intention to take a journey and buying a ticket; absolute bodhichitta is like actually being a traveler. In the same way, we buy our ticket first and fly later.

The ceremony of taking the bodhisattva vow is also an acknowledgment of our potential for enlightenment. It inspires us to recognize that we have bodhichitta in us already. So in taking the bodhisattva vow we are expanding our vision infinitely, beyond this little square world of ours. In a sense, it is like a heart transplant. We are replacing our old heart, which is oriented toward ego and self-aggrandizement, with a new heart characterized by compassion and a larger vision.

The quality that makes this transplant possible is our own gentleness. So in a sense this new heart has been present all along. It is simply rediscovered within the old heart, as in peeling an onion. That discovery of bodhichitta is extremely powerful. Since we have basic generosity and compassion within ourselves, we do not have to borrow from anybody else. Based on that inherent quality of wakefulness, we can act directly, on the spot.

Often our sense of vulnerability, our feeling that we need to protect ourselves, acts as an obstacle to any sense of warmth. But on the bodhisattva path we take chances, extending ourselves without reservation for the sake of others. And it is the discovery of our own wakefulness, or bodhichitta, that creates the trust that allows us to take such chances. Such wakefulness, once acknowledged, develops constantly and cannot be destroyed. As long as such warmth and sympathy exist within us we are like food for flies; opportunities for expressing our warmth come upon us like swarms of flies. It is as though we magnetically attract such situations to ourselves. And this is our chance not to reject them but to work with them.

When we begin to give up personal territory, automatically there is some sense of awakeness, or gap in conceptualization, in our hearts. We begin to develop friendliness toward the world. At that point we can no longer blame society or the weather or the mosquitoes for anything. We have to take personal responsibility, blaming not the world but ourselves, rightly or wrongly. It is our duty to do so. There is no point in creating endless cosmic court cases as to who is right and who is wrong. Nobody wins, and such cases will only escalate into cosmic battles, a third world war. So somebody has to begin somewhere: the person taking the bodhisattva vow has to make the first move. Otherwise there is no beginning of generosity and no end of chaos and aggression. In fact, on the bodhisattva path, such nonaggression becomes one's total view of the world.

Giving Up Privacy

We cannot have personal pleasure once we launch onto the bodhisattva path. We cannot reserve a little area just for ourselves. Usually keeping something back for ourselves is very important. But in this case there is no personal privilege or pleasure. Of course we would still like to have a little corner to ourselves; we would like to shut the door and play a little music or read a novel or *Time* magazine or perhaps study Buddhism. But those days are gone. From the time we take the bodhisattva vow, there is no privacy. In fact a personal reference point of any kind is needless at this point. We have been sold to sentient beings, merchandised. Sentient beings can plow on us, shit on us, sow seeds on our back—use us like the earth. And it is very, very dangerous and irritating to no longer have any privacy.

It is interesting that we could be totally public persons, twenty-four hours a day. Even when we fall asleep we could still be doing something—we are completely dedicated. With such a commitment, we no longer ask for vacations. If we ask for a vacation, or a break from that public world, it is a little fishy: we are still trying to preserve the little corner that we personally control, which is one of our biggest problems. In taking the bodhisattva vow, we are finally giving up privacy at the crude level, but we are also giving up privacy within ourselves. Our minds are usually somewhat schizophrenic: one aspect would like to keep itself hidden from the other aspects. But we are giving that up as well. So in whatever a bodhisattva does there is no privacy, no secrecy. In other words, we are not leading double lives any more; we are leading a single life dedicated to practice as well as to helping other beings. That does not mean that we become miniature gurus or masters controlling other people. Instead of being big currents in the ocean, we may be just little drops. If we become too ambitious, we may become too egotistical. So we should watch ourselves. Sitting meditation provides immense help in this regard. It shows us that we can simply be completely open and awake, realizing that the world we live in is not our personal world but a shared one.

Refugees and Bodhisattvas

Entering the bodhisattva path is very demanding—much more demanding than being a refugee. When we took the refuge vow, we committed ourselves to the path. We were inspired by the buddhadharma, and we knew that we were not going to cop out. Because we developed some understanding of our basic nature, we became strong, disciplined people, no longer nuisances to the rest of society. But, at the same time, the path of individual salvation, or individual commitment, was not completely fulfilling. Something was missing: we had not yet worked with other people, other sentient beings. Having taken the refuge vow, strong messages began to come to us that our commitment to sentient beings had not yet been fulfilled. Our whole approach seemed to become an ingrown toenail: we were eating ourselves up rather than expanding and working with others.

Having prepared the ground with the refuge vow, having given up everything, we begin to be inspired to relate with the world. We have put our own situation in order. If we had not already developed some compassion and openness toward ourselves, we could make no headway at all. But having done that, we are still not completely free. In order to develop further, we need to be energized; we need to take another leap of some kind, which is the bodhisattva vow. But this does not mean we are already bodhisattvas. In fact, we are barely ready to take the vow. But since we have responsibilities to the world, we can no longer sit back and sulk about our own negativities and upheavals. At the same time that such things are happening with ourselves, we have to go out and work with other people. We may have a wound on our foot, but we can still try to support somebody else. That is the style of the bodhisattva path: our own inconvenience is not considered all that important. At the bodhisattva level, not only are we travelers on the path but we are also spokesmen for the enlightened attitude, which means giving up self-indulgence altogether.

Bodhisattva Activity

The bodhisattva's way of relating to others is expressed in the phrase "inviting all sentient beings as one's guests." By treating someone as a guest we view our relationship with him as important. We offer our guests specially cooked food with special hospitality. There is also a sense that our relationship to our guest is impermanent; our guest is going to leave. Therefore there is constant appreciation and a sense that this is a very opportune time. So the life of a bodhisattva is one of seeing everyone as one's guest, constantly. And that notion of inviting all sentient beings as guests is the starting point of compassion.

Compassion is the heart of the practice of meditation-in-action, or bodhisattva activity. It happens as a sudden glimpse—simultaneous awareness and warmth. Looking at it fully, it is a threefold process: a sense of warmth in oneself, a sense of seeing through confusion, and a sense of openness. But this whole process happens very abruptly. There is no time to analyze. There is no time to walk out or to hold on. There is not even time to refer back, to note that "I am doing this."

A bodhisattva's activity is both energetic and gentle. We have enough power to exert our energy, but at the same time there is the gentleness to change our decisions to suit the situation. Such gentle, energetic activity is based on knowledge: we are aware of the situation around us, but we are also aware of our version of the situation—what we want to do. Every aspect is seen clearly.

Having taken the bodhisattva vow, we may feel somewhat hesitant to act on our inspiration. Looked at generally, the situations we find ourselves in seem illogical and confusing. But once we look at our everyday life in the definite way of ongoing practice, our actions can become much more clear-cut: when there is a pull toward ego we can cut through that tendency; when there is hesitation about going beyond our egocentric perspective we can let go. Our hesitation may be that we are afraid we may not make the right decision, that we don't know what to do. But we can push ourselves into the situation so that the proper direction comes about naturally. We may be slightly fearful of the consequences of our action, somewhat tentative in our approach. But at the same time there is confidence, the inspiration to deal with things properly. That combined mentality of confidence and tentativeness comprises skillful action.

In a sense, taking the bodhisattva vow is a tremendous pretense. We are uncertain that we are able to tread on the bodhisattva path, but we still decide to do it. That leap is necessary in developing basic confidence. The situations we encounter in our everyday lives are both solid and workable. We don't have to shy away from them, nor do we have to exaggerate them by rolling in like a tank. We work with each situation simply and directly, as it happens.

This kind of bodhisattva activity is traditionally described in terms of the six *paramitas,* or transcendental virtues: generosity, discipline, patience, exertion, meditation, and transcendental knowledge.

The paramita of *generosity* is particularly connected with the notion of sharing knowledge, or teaching. In fact, everybody who takes the bodhisattva vow is regarded as a potential teacher. If out of paranoia, embarrassment, or a sense that we want to possess our knowledge we refuse to teach, we are abandoning sentient beings. Even if we feel we are not up to becoming teachers, we should be prepared to become apprentice teachers. We should be willing to share what we know with others. At the same time, we have to control ourselves to the extent that we do not share something we do *not* know.

In the bodhisattva ceremony, we express our generosity by making an offering to the three jewels: the Buddha, the dharma, and the sangha. Fundamentally, we are offering our own ego: we are offering our sense of sanity to the Buddha, our keen perception of the nature of the path to the dharma, and our sense of companionship to the sangha.

A traditional way of developing generosity is to offer our food to someone else. Even if we are hungry, we hold our plate of food in our hands and give it away mentally before eating. At that very moment of giving something away, we are actually beginning to practice the paramitas. By giving away something personal and significant in our lives, we are helping to clarify our attachments and to overcome the habitual pattern of spiritual materialism. And in fact, we are also abandoning the attainment of enlightenment at that point.

The paramita of *discipline,* or morality, is based on a sense of trust in oneself. In contrast, traditional morality is often based on a lack of trust and a fear of one's own aggressive impulses. When we have such little confidence in our own intelligence and wakefulness, so-called immoral persons pose a tremendous threat to us. For instance, when we reject a murderer as an immoral person it might be because of our fear that we might murder somebody as well. Or we might even be afraid to hold a gun, which represents death and killing, thinking that we might shoot ourselves on the spot. In other words, we do not trust ourselves or our own generosity. That obsession with our own inadequacies is one of the biggest obstacles on the bodhisattva path. If we feel we are inadequate bodhisattvas, we do not make good bodhisattvas at all. In fact, that obsession with a moralistic, guilt-ridden approach is a form of being trapped in the hinayana perspective. It is an attempt to confirm one's ego. The sense of trust in oneself allows the bodhisattva to work skillfully with whatever is happening, to the point of being willing to commit immorality out of compassion for sentient beings. This is obviously quite delicate, but it fundamentally involves trying to work with people in an intelligent way.

Bodhisattva discipline arises from a sense of trust in oneself, but it also involves arousing trust in others. There is a sense of heroism, of raising the banner of sanity and proclaiming an open way. If we are too mousy or small, we do not know who we are or with whom we are communicating. There is still a feeling of territoriality, of keeping things to ourselves. And since we base our trust on some feeling of being special, we are afraid of arousing the confidence of those around us. We do not want to destroy our own petty base of power. In contrast, the bodhisattva path is expansive—a great vision of openness in which there is tremendous room to work with people without one-upsmanship or impatience. Since our vision is not dependent on maintaining ego, we cannot be threatened. We have nothing to lose, so we can actually give an inch in our relations with people.

The paramita of *patience* is the willingness to work with our own emotions through the practice of meditation. This in turn allows us to begin to work peacefully with others. Usually we don't want to work with aggressive people because we feel they will not give us an easy time. They are a threat to our unbodhisattvalike mentality of looking for pleasure and security. And when we encounter somebody who wrongs us, we harbor tremendous resentment and refuse to forgive him. Our tendency is always to view such aggressive people, rather than our attitude of holding back, as the problem. But the paramita of patience requires that we stop the ego-centered approach of always blaming others. Quite simply, the practice of patience means not returning threats, anger, attacks, or insults. But this does not mean being purely passive. Instead we use the other person's energy, as in judo. Since we have related to our own aggression through the practice of meditation, we are not threatened by the other person's aggression, nor do we need to respond impulsively or aggressively. Our response is self-defensive in the sense that we do not return such a person's threat, and at the same time, we prevent further aggression by allowing the other person's own energy to undercut itself.

The paramita of *exertion* involves being willing to work hard for the sake of others. Tremendous energy comes from overcoming the emotional complications and conceptual frivolity of one's mind, which usually provides an excuse for avoiding bodhisattva activity. We no longer indulge our laziness and self-centeredness by dwelling on the familiarity and

snugness of our own emotional complications. The bodhisattva is inspired to overcome such laziness by developing
simplicity. Such simplicity arises from a perspective of spaciousness in which we do not need to manipulate our emotions in any way or to get rid of them by acting them out;
instead we can deal directly with them as they arise. In this
way emotions are no longer obstacles but a source of further
energy.

In addition to our emotions, our minds also have a conceptualizing quality, which seems to be a combination of
panic and logical reasoning. We are constantly insecure, and
therefore we are constantly trying to reassure ourselves. Our
minds have the ability to produce hundreds of answers, hundreds of reasons to assure ourselves that what we are doing is
right. And when we teach, we impose this conceptualizing
chatter on others. In order to justify ourselves in such a situation, we talk a lot, trying to con our students. The bodhisattva is able to see this tremendously complicated structure
of ongoing self-confirming chatter. Having overcome the laziness of emotional indulgence through simplicity, the bodhisattva is also able to see through the conceptual super-
structure arising out of the emotions. To the bodhisattva,
neither the emotions nor conceptual mind is seen as an obstacle. In fact, nothing is regarded as an obstacle, and nothing is regarded as evil or bad. Everything is simply part of
the landscape of the bodhisattva's journey. So the bodhisattva sees his or her life as one continuous venture—the
perpetual discovery of new understanding. And since his notion of path is not restricted in any way, there is the development of tremendous energy and a willingness to work very
hard. So the paramita of exertion is not a project; it is the
natural and spontaneous expression of the vastness of the
bodhisattva's vision.

In practicing the paramita of *meditation*, we relate to meditation as a natural process; it is neither an obstacle nor a particular virtue. If we become impatient with constant thought-chattering in our meditation practice, we may avoid meditating. We had been expecting a comfortably rewarding situation, so we are unwilling to work with the irritations that constantly come up—we can't be bothered. On the other hand, we might get very attached to how good a meditator we are. Any kind of blissful experience we regard as some form of divine grace, as proof that what we are doing makes sense. We feel we can meditate better and more than anybody else. In this case, we view our meditation practice as a contest for the championship. But whether we try to avoid sitting practice or become attached to it as some sort of self-confirmation, we are still avoiding the paramita of meditation, which is a willingness to work unceasingly with our own neurosis and speed.

The paramita of *transcendental knowledge* is a quality of interest in the teachings that is nondogmatic and not based on furthering the development of ego. From the point of view of transcendental knowledge, any gesture based on developing ego or taking the easy way out is heretical. Such heresy is not a question of theism or atheism, but of preaching the language of ego, even if it is done in the name of buddhadharma. Even while practicing the mahayana, we may still be looking for a self as our basic being: "There's still some hope, I can develop tremendous muscles. I can develop tremendous lungs. I can show you that I can control my mind even though I believe in the mahayana tradition." But that double-agent approach is extremely stupid and unworkable.

It is possible for us to become so attached to the mahayana perspective that we renounce and disparage hinayana. But without the discipline of hinayana there is no basis for the development of mahayana. On the other hand, we may become very dogmatic and attached solely to hinayana. This

seems to be an expression of our cowardice: we are not willing to step onto the wide-open path of mahayana. In contrast to these dogmatic extremes, the paramita of transcendental knowledge has a perky quality of interest in the
intellectual logic of all three yanas: hinayana, mahayana, and
vajrayana. This interest and curiosity is not purely intellectual but is based on the practice of meditation.

Basically, the idea of bodhisattva activity is to have good
manners. In spite of our own irritation we should be able to
extend our hospitality to others. This is quite different from
hypocritical hospitality. Rather, it is an expression of enlightenment; it is a working state of mind in which we extend hospitality beyond our irritations.

It is perhaps most important in working with others that
we do not develop *idiot compassion*, which means always trying to be kind. Since this superficial kindness lacks courage
and intelligence, it does more harm than good. It is as
though a doctor, out of apparent kindness, refuses to treat
his patient because the treatment might be painful, or as
though a mother cannot bear the discomfort of disciplining
her child. Unlike idiot compassion, real compassion is not
based on a simple-minded avoidance of pain. Real compassion is uncompromising in its allegiance to basic sanity.
People who distort the path—that is, people who are working against the development of basic sanity—should be cut
through on the spot if need be. That is extremely important. There is no room for idiot compassion. We should try
to cut through as much self-deception as possible in order to
teach others as well as ourselves. So the final cop-out of a
bodhisattva is when, having already achieved everything else,
he is unable to go beyond idiot compassion.

Taking the bodhisattva vow has tremendous power for the
very reason that it is not something we do just for the pleasure of ego. It is beyond oneself. Taking the vow is like

planting the seed of a fast-growing tree, whereas something done for the benefit of ego is like sowing a grain of sand. Planting such a seed as the bodhisattva vow undermines ego and leads to a tremendous expansion of perspective. Such heroism, or bigness of mind, fills all of space completely, utterly, absolutely. Within such a vast perspective, nothing is claustrophobic and nothing is intimidating. There is only the vast idea of unceasingly helping all sentient beings, as limitless as space, along the path to enlightenment.

The Bodhisattva Vow Ceremony

Taking the bodhisattva vow is a public statement of your intention to embark on the bodhisattva path. Simply acknowledging that intention to yourself is not enough. You have to be brave enough to say it in front of others. In so doing, you are taking a big chance, but you are going to go ahead with it anyway.

To begin the ceremony, you request the teacher to give the bodhisattva vow and to accept you into the family of the Buddha by saying: "May the teacher be gracious to me. Just as the former tathagatas, arhants, samyaksambuddhas, exalted ones, and bodhisattvas living at the level of the great bhumis developed an attitude directed toward unsurpassable, perfect great enlightenment, so also I request the teacher to help me in developing such an attitude." The teacher responds by instructing you, as his disciple, to renounce samsara and to develop compassion for sentient beings, desire for enlightenment, devotion to the Three Jewels, and respect for the teacher. He reminds you to deepen the feeling of compassion and to plant it firmly in your heart, since "sentient beings are as limitless as celestial space and as long as there are sentient beings they will be affected by conflicting emotions, which will cause them to do evil, for which in turn they will suffer."

This ceremony is magical: the bodhisattvas of the past, present, and future are present, watching you. At this point you prostrate three times to these people, as well as to your own conscience. In doing these three prostrations, you bind yourself to the earth and reacknowledge your basic state of homelessness.

You then begin the actual vow by saying: "From now on, until I have become the very quintessence of enlightenment, I will develop an attitude directed toward unsurpassable, perfect great enlightenment so that the beings who have not crossed over may do so, who have not yet been delivered may be so, who have not yet found relief may find it, and who have not yet passed into nirvana may do so."

The discipline at this point in the ceremony is to identify with the elements, which nurture all sentient beings. You are becoming mother earth; therefore, you will have to accommodate all sorts of pokings and proddings and dumping of garbage—but in fact you are delighted by the whole thing. At this point you read a passage from *The Bodhicharyavatara* by Shantideva that expresses this process quite beautifully: "As earth and other elements, together with space, eternally provide sustenance in many ways for the countless sentient beings, so may I become sustenance in every way for sentient beings to the limits of space until all have attained nirvana."

Now that you have given yourself to others, you are not going to be resentful. Sometimes after a guest has arrived and you are offering him your hospitality, you may have a sense of regretting that you ever invited him. Or you may remember that as a child you sometimes found your parents' hospitality very claustrophobic and annoying: "I wish Daddy wouldn't invite those strangers over. I like my privacy." But from the point of view of a bodhisattva, your parents' example is fantastic. You are committing yourself to that kind of hospitality, and you are willing to admit people into your space. In doing so you are following the example of former bodhisattvas who also committed themselves to basic generosity, intelligence, and enlightenment. So with that in mind, you repeat: "As the sugatas of old gave birth to the bodhichitta and progressively established themselves in the discipline of a bodhisattva, so I too, for the benefit of beings, shall give birth to the bodhichitta and progressively train myself in that discipline."

Next, you offer a gift as an expression of generosity and further commitment. Even if the gift is a corpse, you are going to present whatever you have as a real gesture of committing yourself to bodhichitta. In giving something about which you care very much, too much—whatever it may be—you are offering your sense of attachment, your basic attitude of clinging.

The presentation of a gift is equivalent to the moment in the refuge vow when the preceptor snaps his fingers. But the reason you don't have the abstract energies of the lineage or of basic Buddhism coming into your system in this case is that the bodhisattva vow is more on the emotional level. Taking refuge is related to the ordinary, moralistic level: your commitment is that you are not going to be unfaithful. The bodhisattva vow is much more subtle: you don't really have a specific moment in which bodhichitta enters into you. But in some way or other, when you give your gift and you are inspired to let go of your clinging and self-centeredness, at that moment you really become a child of the Buddha, a bodhisattva. At that point, whether you like it or not, you take on a heavy burden—which is happily unavoidable. You cannot undo it. In the case of hinayana, you can give up your vow, but you cannot give up your bodhisattva vow, even after lives and lives. You cannot give it up because the discipline of mahayana is not based on physical existence but on conscience, in the very ordinary sense.

Having offered your gift, you can appreciate what you have done. Realizing that you have not made a mistake you say: "At this moment my birth has become fruitful, I have realized my human life. Today I am born into the family of the Buddha. Now I am a child of the Buddha."

The next passage you recite gives all kinds of examples of how you can be helpful to society and to the world—how you can live with yourself and with other sentient beings: "From now on I will forthrightly perform the actions befitting to my family. I will act so as not to degrade the faultlessness and discipline of my family. Just as with a blind man finding a jewel in a heap of dust, thus, somehow, bodhichitta has been born in me. This is the supreme amrita which destroys death, the inexhaustible treasure which removes the world's poverty; it is the supreme medicine which cures the world's sickness, the tree which provides rest for beings weary of wandering on the paths of existence; it is the universal bridge on which all travelers may pass over the lower realms, the rising moon of mind which dispels the torment of the klesas; it is the great sun which puts an end to the obscurity of ignorance, the pure butter which comes of churning the milk of holy dharma. For travelers wandering on the paths of existence seeking happiness from objects of enjoyment, it is supreme bliss near at hand, the great feast which satisfies sentient beings."

Now you are ready to receive your bodhisattva name. The name you receive symbolizes generosity in working with others. It is not a further means of building up your territory or identity, but an expression of nonego. You are no longer yours, but you belong to others. Bodhisattva names are more powerful than refuge names because there is more need of being reminded to work with others than of being reminded to work on yourself. Your bodhisattva name is an expression of your subtle style: somebody could insult you by using it; somebody could encourage you by using it. It expresses a more sensitive area than the refuge name, which is extremely useful. In other words, your bodhisattva name acts as a password; it is a very accurate guideline to your particular style of basic openness in working with all sentient beings. Both your potentialities and your basic attributes are expressed in your bodhisattva name, which should be recalled whenever a critical situation comes up. Instead of looking to a savior, you should remember your name as a reminder of the solidness of your involvement on the bodhisattva path. It is a token that you have made a link with your buddha-nature, *tathagatagarbha*: you have dug a well and found fresh water which you can use continuously. Your bodhisattva name represents your commitment to basic sanity, your willingness to devote your life to all sentient beings. Therefore it is very powerful and important.

Without any doubt, having taken the bodhisattva vow, you should celebrate. Taking the vow is a landmark, not just a casual thing. It is something extraordinary, something historic. Keeping that in mind, you invite everyone to share your joy that you finally have become a worker for all sentient beings, by saying: "Today, witnessed by all the protectors, I have welcomed the sentient beings and sugatas. Devas and asuras rejoice!"

That ends the bodhisattva vow ceremony. It is a simple ceremony that presents you with the extreme challenge of committing yourself to people without consideration for your own comfort. And the key to meeting such a challenge is fearlessness. By taking the vow you therefore enter the fearless world of the warrior.

7

Sacred Outlook:
The Practice of Vajrayogini

"Experiencing the vajra mind of Vajrayogini is so deep and vast that if thoughts arise, they do not become highlights: they are small fish in a huge ocean of space."

The *vajrayana,* the *tantric* teaching of the Buddha, contains tremendous magic and power. Its magic lies in its ability to transform confusion and neurosis into awakened mind and to reveal the everyday world as a sacred realm. Its power is that of unerring insight into the true nature of phenomena and of seeing through ego and its deceptions.

According to the tantric tradition, the vajrayana is regarded as the complete teaching of the Buddha: it is the path of complete discipline, complete surrender, and complete liberation. It is important to realize, however, that the vajrayana is firmly grounded in the basic teachings of the *sutrayana,* the teachings of egolessness and compassion.

Frequently, the exceptional strength and efficacy of the vajrayana are misunderstood as a promise of instant enlight-

Written to accompany a 1983 exhibit of Himalayan Buddhist art.

enment. But one cannot become enlightened overnight; in fact, it is highly deceptive and even dangerous to think in such a way. Without exception, the Buddhist teachings point to the erroneous belief in a self, or ego, as the cause of suffering and the obstacle to liberation. All of the great teachers of the past practiced the preliminary meditative disciplines diligently before becoming students of the vajrayana. Without this basic training in the practice of meditation, there is no ground from which to work with the vajrayana at all.

The *Vajrayogini* principle, as it has been experienced, understood, and transmitted by the gurus of the Karma Kagyü lineage of Tibet, to which I belong, is part of the vajrayana tradition. I feel very honored to have the opportunity to explain the Vajrayogini principle and the shrine connected with Vajrayogini practice. At the same time, I have a responsibility to the lineage, as well as to the reader, to introduce Vajrayogini properly.

Egolessness and Compassion

A brief discussion of fundamental Buddhism as well as of the *mahayana* path is necessary here so that it will be clearly understood that Vajrayogini is not to be perceived as an external deity or force. This is sometimes rather difficult for Westerners to understand because of the Judeo-Christian belief in God. Buddhism is a nontheistic religion; there is no belief in an external savior. Nontheism is synonymous with the realization of *egolessness,* which is first discovered through the practices of *shamatha* and *vipashyana* meditation.

In *shamatha* meditation, we work with breath and posture as expressions of our state of being. By assuming a dignified and upright posture and identifying with the outgoing breath, we begin to make friends with ourselves in a funda-

mental sense. When thoughts arise, they are not treated as
enemies, but they are included in the practice and labeled
simply as "thinking." *Shamatha* in Sanskrit, or *shiné* in Tibetan, means "dwelling in a state of peace." Through shamatha practice one begins to see the simplicity of one's original state of mind and to see how confusion, speed, and
aggression are generated by ignoring the peacefulness of
one's being. This is the first experience of egolessness, in
which one realizes the transparency of fixed ideas about oneself and the illusoriness of what one thinks of as "I" or
"me."

With further practice, we begin to lose the reference
point of self-consciousness, and we experience the environment of practice and the world without bringing everything
back to the narrow viewpoint of "me." We begin to be interested in "that," rather than purely being interested in
"this." The development of perception that is penetrating
and precise without reference to oneself is called *vipashyana*
in Sanskrit and *lhakthong* in Tibetan, which means "clear
seeing." The technique of vipashyana does not differ from
shamatha; rather, vipashyana grows out of the continued application of shamatha practice. The clear seeing, or insight,
of vipashyana sees that there is no more of a solid existence
in phenomena than there is in oneself, so that we begin to
realize the egolessness of "other." We also begin to see that
suffering in the world is caused by clinging to erroneous
conceptions about self and phenomena. We perceive that
philosophical, psychological, and religious ideas of eternity
and external liberation are myths created by ego-mind. So,
in vipashyana practice, egolessness is the recognition of fundamental aloneness, the nontheistic realization that we cannot look for help outside of ourselves.

Altogether, the ground of Buddhist practice is called the
path of "individual liberation," which is *pratimoksha* in San-

skirt and *sosor tharpa* in Tibetan. By practicing the disciplines of shamatha and vipashyana, both in meditation and throughout one's life, we can actually liberate ourselves from personal confusion and neurosis and free ourselves from causing harm to ourselves and others. We become inspired to commit ourselves fully to this path by taking refuge in the Buddha (as the example of a human being who attained enlightenment by renouncing external help and working with his own mind), in the *dharma* (the teachings of egolessness that can be heard and experienced), and in the *sangha* (the community of practitioners who follow the path of the Buddha by practicing as he did). We realize that in this spinning world of confused existence we have had the rare good fortune to encounter the true path of liberation.

The *mahayana,* or "great vehicle," goes beyond the inspiration of individual liberation. On the whole, the mahayana approach is basically one of working for the benefit of others with whatever the world presents; therefore, it is an endless journey. As we embark on this journey without destination, our preconceptions begin to fall away. This experience of non-reference point, which initially could be just a momentary flash in one's mind, is the first glimpse of *shunyata.* *Shunya* means "empty," and *ta* makes it "empti*ness*." According to tradition, shunyata is empty of "I" and empty of "other"; it is absolutely empty. This experience of emptiness is realizing that there is no "I" as actor, no action, and no "other" to be acted upon.

Shunyata is not the nihilistic idea of nothingness, or voidness. It is the complete absence of grasping and fixation— the complete egolessness of subject and object. It is therefore the absence of separation between self and other.

The experience of shunyata provides tremendous room and tremendous vision. There is room because we see that there is no obstacle to going out, to expanding. And there is vision because there is no separation between oneself and one's experience. We can perceive things clearly, as they are, without filters of any kind. This unbiased perception is called *prajna*, or "discriminating awareness." Prajna is the sharpness of the perception of shunyata and the knowledge that comes from that perception.

In fact, *prajna* literally means "superior knowledge" or "best knowledge." The highest knowledge that one can have is the knowledge of egoless insight, which begins as the experience of vispashyana and matures in the mahayana into prajna. The discriminating awareness of prajna sees that "I" and "other" are not separate and, therefore, that the enlightenment of oneself and the enlightenment of others cannot be separated.

In this way, the perception of shunyata makes us altogether more wakeful and compassionate. We feel immense interest in others and immense caring for others, whose suffering is not different from our own. This is the beginning of the mahayana practice of *exchanging oneself for others*.

The notion of exchange means giving whatever assistance is needed; we extend our kindness, sanity, and love to other people. In exchange, we are willing to take on others' pain, confusion, and hypocrisy. We are willing to take the blame for any problems that might come up—not because we wish to be martyrs, but because we feel that there is an infinite reservoir of goodness and sanity to share. At the mahayana level, egolessness is expanded into the path of selfless action, which goes completely beyond ego-clinging. It is this surrendering of ego, which we shall discuss later, that makes it possible to enter the vajrayana path.

Vajra Nature and the Yidam Principle

When we let go of grasping and fixation completely, we are able to rest in the intrinsic goodness of our minds, and we regard whatever discursive thoughts that arise—passion, aggression, delusion, or any conflicting emotions—as merely ripples in the pond of mind. Out of that, we begin to realize that there is a greater vision beyond grasping and fixation. That vision is very firm and definite. It is not definite in the style of ego, but it is like the sun, which shines all the time. When we fly in an airplane above the clouds, we realize that the sun is always shining even when it is cloudy and rainy below. In the same way, when we cease to hold onto our identity, our ego, we begin to see that the nonexistence of ego is a powerful, real, and indestructible state of being. We realize that, like the sun, it is a continuous situation which does not wax or wane.

This state of being is called *vajra nature*. *Vajra,* or *dorjé* in Tibetan, means "indestructible," or "having the qualities of a diamond." Vajra nature is the tough, immovable quality of egolessness, which is the basis for the vajrayana path. The term *vajrayana* itself means "vehicle of indestructibility"— the *"vajra* vehicle." The vajrayana is also called the *tantrayana,* or "tantric vehicle." *Tantra,* or *gyü* in Tibetan, means "continuity" or "thread." Vajra nature is the continuity of egolessness, or wakefulness, which, like the sun, is brilliant and all-pervasive.

The deities of the vajrayana are embodiments of vajra nature. In particular, the deities called *yidams* are important for the practice of vajrayana. The best translation of *yidam* that I have found is "personal deity." Actually, *yidam* is a shortened form of the phrase *yi-kyi tamtsik,* which means "sacred bondage of one's mind." *Yi* means "mind," *kyi* means "of," and *tamtsik* means "sacred word" or "sacred bondage." *Tamtsik,* which in Sanskrit is *samaya,* will become important in a later discussion of the sacred commitments of the vajrayana. *Mind* here refers to vajra nature, the basic sanity and wakefulness of one's being, freed from ego-clinging.

The *yidam* is the manifestation of this enlightened mind; it is the *yidam* who connects, or binds, the practitioner to the enlightened sanity within himself. So, according to the tantric understanding, the yidam is a nontheistic deity who embodies one's innate vajra nature, rather than any form of external help.

There are many thousands of tantric deities, but in the Karma Kagyü lineage, Vajrayogini is a particularly important yidam. When a student has completed the preliminary vajrayana practices, called the *ngöndro,* he receives *abhisheka,* or empowerment, to begin yidam practice, in which he identifies with a personal deity as the embodiment of his innate wakefulness, or vajra nature. In the Karma Kagyü tradition, Vajrayogini is the first yidam given to a student. In order to understand the Vajrayogini principle in any depth, a discussion of the stages of vajrayana practice through which a student is introduced to the yidam is necessary.

Devotion

In the Buddhist tradition, relating to a teacher is not hero worship; the teacher is appreciated as an example of living dharma. When entering the Buddhist path, the practitioner respects the teacher as a wise man or elder. The teacher in the mahayana is called the *kalyanamitra,* or "spiritual friend"—he is a friend in the sense that he is willing to share one's life completely and to walk with one on the path. He is truly an example of the mahayana practice of exchanging oneself for others.

At the vajrayana level, we begin with faith in the teachings and the teacher, because we have already experienced the truth and the workability of the teachings for ourselves. Then, with the discovery of vajra nature, faith begins to develop into devotion, which is *mögü* in Tibetan. *Mö* means "longing," and *gü* means "respect." We develop tremendous respect for the teacher and a longing for what he can impart because we see that he is the embodiment of vajra nature, the embodiment of wakeful mind. At this level, the teacher becomes the guru. He is the vajra master—the one who has mastered vajra truth, indestructible truth, and who can transmit that vajra power to others. However, the vajrayana can be extremely destructive if we are not properly prepared to receive these teachings. Therefore, in order to practice the vajrayana, we must have a relationship with a vajra master, who completely understands the practitioner and the practice and who knows how to bring the two together.

One's relationship with the vajra master involves surrendering oneself to the teacher as the final expression of egolessness. This allows the practitioner to develop fully the threefold vajra nature: vajra body, vajra speech, and vajra mind. The maturation of devotion into complete surrendering is called *loté lingkyur* in Tibetan. *Loté* means "trust," *ling* means "completely," and *kyur* means "abandoning" or "letting go." So *loté lingkyur* means "to trust completely and let go"—to abandon one's ego completely. Without such surrender, there is no way to give up the last vestiges of ego; nor could the teacher introduce the yidam, the essence of egolessness. In fact, without such devotion to the teacher, one might attempt to use the vajrayana teachings to rebuild the fortress of ego.

Ngöndro

In order to develop proper devotion and surrender, a student of the vajrayana begins with the practice of *ngöndro*, the foundation practices that are preliminary to receiving abhisheka. *Ngön* means "before," and *dro* means "going." In the Karma Kagyü lineage, there are five practices that make up ngöndro: prostrations, the recitation of the refuge vow, the *Vajrasattva mantra* practice, the *mandala* offering, and the practice of *guru-yoga*. These are called the *extraordinary foundations*. Ngöndro is the means of connecting oneself with the wisdom of the guru and the guru's lineage. In prostrations, as the starting point, one is humbling oneself and expressing one's gratitude for the example of the vajra master and the lineage forefathers. One visualizes the gurus of the lineage, including one's own guru, in the form of the primordial buddha. Over the course of many practice sessions, the practitioner prostrates to the lineage 108,000 times while reciting the refuge vow 108,000 times. In that way, one reaffirms one's commitment to the basic path of discipline and renunciation and, at the same time, expresses surrender to the vajrayana teachings and the vajra master. Through prostrations, one catches one's first glimpse of the lineage.

Mantra practice leads to a closer experience of the lineage wisdom. It allows one to work directly with obstacles and psychological obscurations and to realize that defilements are temporary and can be overcome. The deity Vajrasattva—literally, "vajra being"—is visualized as a youthful white prince who is both the essence of vajra wisdom and the wisdom body of one's guru. In contrast, the practitioner's own body is visualized as being filled with impurities of all kinds: physical, mental, and emotional. While reciting the mantra of Vajrasattva 108,000 times, one visualizes that one's body is slowly cleansed of these impurities by the action of Vajrasattva. By the end of a practice period, one visualizes oneself as possessing the same pure nature as Vajrasattva. The point of mantra practice, therefore, is to recognize one's inherent purity.

In mandala practice, one gives oneself and one's world as an offering to the lineage. The student offers 108,000 mandalas made from heaps of saffron-scented rice mixed with jewels and other precious substances. While constructing the mandala, one visualizes the world and everything in it—all its wealth and beauty and one's myriad sense perceptions—as an offering to the gurus and buddhas, who are visualized before one. The practitioner's sense of pure being should also be included in the offering and given up; this is called "giving up the giver." When one gives up so completely, there is no one left to watch what is being given, and no one to appreciate how generous one is being. The more one surrenders in this way, the more richness one develops. There is never a problem of running out of things to offer. One's human life is in itself an immensely rich situation to offer to the lineage.

Having completed the mandala offerings one then practices guru-yoga, which is like actually meeting the guru face-to-face for the first time. Guru-yoga is the first opportunity to receive the *adhishthana,* or blessings, of the guru's wisdom.

In guru-yoga, the practitioner begins to realize the nondual nature of devotion: there is no separation between the lineage and oneself and, in fact, the vajra being of the guru is a reflection of one's own innate nature. In this way, the practice of ngöndro, culminating in guru-yoga, helps to overcome theistic notions about the teacher or about the vajrayana itself. One realizes that the lineage is not an entity outside of oneself: one is not worshiping the teacher or his ancestors as gods. Rather, one is connecting with *vajra* sanity, which is so powerful because of its nonexistence—its utter egolessness.

Sacred Outlook

When we begin to mix our minds with the energy of the lineage, we are not doing so in order to protect ourselves from the world. In fact, devotion brings us closer to our experience, to our world. As a result of the practice of ngöndro, we feel a greater sense of warmth and gentleness in ourselves. Because of that, we can relax and take a fresh look at the phenomenal world. We find that life can be an easy, natural process. Because there is no need to struggle, we start to experience goodness everywhere: we experience a tremendous sense of freedom and sacredness is everything.

When we experience this self-existing sacredness, we realize that the only way to abide continuously in this state of freedom is to enter completely into the guru's world, because such freedom is the blessing of the guru. It was the guru who presented the practice that led to the experience of freedom, and it is the guru who manifests the epitome of this freedom. In fact, we begin to see that the self-existing sacredness of the world is simultaneously an expression of the guru. This experience is known as *sacred outlook,* or *tag nang* in Tibetan. *Tag nang* literally means "pure perception." The idea of purity here refers to an absence of imprisonment. Sacred outlook means perceiving the world and oneself as intrinsically good and unconditionally free.

The Five Buddha Families

Having developed sacred outlook it is possible to take a further step into the vajra world. When we experience the self-existing sacredness of reality, the vajrayana iconography begins to make sense; it makes sense to picture the world as a sacred realm, as a mandala of enlightened mind. From the viewpoint of sacred outlook, the phenomenal world is seen in terms of five styles of energy: *buddha, vajra, padma, ratna,* and *karma.* Oneself and the people one meets, the seasons, the elements—all aspects of the phenomenal world—are made up of one or more of these styles, or *buddha families.* In tantric iconography, the buddha families make up a mandala with buddha in the center, and vajra, ratna, padma, and karma at the four cardinal points.

One or more of the buddha families can be used to describe a person's intrinsic perspective or stance in the world. Each buddha family principle can have either a neurotic or an enlightened expression. The particular neurosis associated with a buddha family is transmuted into its wisdom, or enlightened, form by the taming process of shamatha-vipashyana meditation, by training in compassion in the mahayana, and, particularly, by the development of sacred outlook in the vajrayana. In their enlightened expression, the buddha families are manifestations of vajra freedom.

The basic quality of *buddha* energy is spaciousness. The confused manifestation of this spacious quality is ignorance, which in this case involves avoiding vivid or unpleasant experience. When buddha energy is transmuted, it becomes the *wisdom of all-encompassing space.* Buddha is associated with the color white and is symbolized by a wheel, which represents this all-encompassing, open nature.

Vajra, which is in the east of the mandala,* is represented by the color blue. The symbol of vajra is a vajra scepter, or *dorje,* whose five prongs pierce the neurosis of ego-mind. The vajra scepter is like a thunderbolt—electric and powerful. Vajra energy is precise and direct. It is the ability to view situations from all possible perspectives and to accurately perceive the details of experience and the larger frameworks in which things take place. The neurotic expressions of vajra energy are aggression and intellectual fixation. When the intellectual accuracy of vajra is transmuted into its enlightened form, it becomes *mirror-like wisdom.* Vajra is associated with

---

*In a traditional mandala, east is at the bottom, south is to the left, west is at the top, and north is to the right.

the element of water. Its neurotic expression, anger, is like clouded, turbulent water; its wisdom aspect is like the clear reflection of a still pond.

The *ratna* family, in the south, is represented by the color yellow. The symbol of the ratna family is a jewel, expressing richness. Ratna energy is like autumn, when fruits and grains are ripe and farmers celebrate the harvest. Ratna is associated with the element of earth, which expresses its solidity and fertility. The neurotic style of ratna is envy or hunger—wanting everything and trying to engulf everything. Its enlightened expression is the *wisdom of equanimity,* because ratna accommodates all experiences and brings out their innate richness. When it is freed from hunger, ratna becomes an expression of powerful expansiveness.

In the west is the *padma* family, which is associated with the color red. The symbol of padma is a lotus, a beautiful, delicate flower which blooms in the mud. Padma is the basic energy of passion, or seduction. Its neurotic aspect is grasping or clinging, which is the confused expression of passion. When passion is freed from fixation on the object of its desire, it becomes *discriminating-awareness wisdom*—the appreciation of every aspect and detail of experience. Padma is associated with the element of fire. In the confused state passion, like fire, does not distinguish among the things it grasps, burns, and destroys. In its enlightened expression, the heat of passion becomes the warmth of compassion.

Karma, in the north of the mandala, is associated with the color green. Its symbol, a sword, represents cutting through hesitation and confusion and accomplishing one's goals accurately and thoroughly. Karma is the *wisdom of all-accomplishing action* in its enlightened manifestation. The neurotic expression of karma energy is resentment and excessive speed. Karma neurosis would like to create a uniform world and resents any sloppiness or inefficiency. When karma is freed from neurosis, it becomes accurate and energetic without resentment or pettiness. Karma is associated with the element of wind, which represents this forceful and energetic quality of action.

Perceiving the energies of the buddha families in people and in situations, we see that confusion is workable and can be transformed into an expression of sacred outlook. The student must reach this understanding before the teacher can introduce the tantric deities, or yidams. Every yidam "belongs" to a buddha family and is "ruler" of the wisdom aspect of that family. The buddha family principles provide a link between ordinary samsaric experience and the brilliance and loftiness of the yidams' world. By understanding the buddha family principles, we can appreciate the tantric deities as embodiments of the energies of sacred world and identify ourselves with that sacredness. With that understanding we can receive abhisheka, or empowerment; we are ready to be introduced to Vajrayogini.

Abhisheka

By receiving the abhisheka of Vajrayogini, the student enters the mandala of Vajrayogini. Through this process, Vajrayogini becomes one's yidam—the embodiment of one's basic being or basic state of mind. *Abhisheka,* which is Sanskrit, literally means "anointment." The Tibetan *wangkur* means "empowerment." The principle of empowerment is that there is a meeting of the minds of the student and vajra master, which is the product of devotion. Because the student is able to open fully to the teacher, the teacher is able to communicate directly the power and wakefulness of the vajrayana through the formal ceremony of abhisheka. In reviewing the history of the Vajrayogini transmission in the

VAJRAYOGINI: THE SOVEREIGN OF DESIRE

VAJRAYOGINI'S SYMBOLIC MEANING

ICONOGRAPHICAL ASPECT	SYMBOLIC OF
a. Hooked Knife	a. Cutting neurotic tendencies. Also the weapon of non-thought.
b. Skull cup filled with amrita	b. Prajna and intoxication of extreme beliefs
c. Staff (khatvanga)	c. Skillful means. The staff is eight-sided, representing the eightfold Aryan Path taught by the Buddha.
1. Scarf	1. The two folds of the scarf represent the inseparability of mahayana and vajrayana.
2. Three skulls	2. The trikaya principle: the top head is a skull representing dharmakaya: the middle head is of a putrefying corpse representing sambhogakaya; the bottom head is a freshly severed head representing nirmanakaya.
d. Sow's head (usually shown over the right ear)	d. Vajra ignorance or nonthought.
e. Hair streaming upwards	e. The wrath of passion. (When Vajrayogini's hair hangs loosely on her shoulders it is a symbol of compassion. Here the emphasis is more on her wrathful aspect.)
f. Crown of five skulls	f. The wisdoms of the five buddha families.
g. Three eyes	g. Knower of the past, present and future. Also Vajrayogini's omniscient vision.

ICONOGRAPHICAL ASPECT	SYMBOLIC OF
h. Wrathful expression, clenching her fangs and biting the lower lip	h. Enraged against the maras.
i. Necklace of freshly severed heads	i. The 51 samskaras, completely liberated in nonthought.
j. One face	j. All dharmas are of one flavor in dharmakaya.
k. Bone ornaments: headdress, earrings, necklace, girdle, anklets and bracelets	k. Perfection of the 5 paramitas of generosity, discipline, patience, exertion, meditation.
l. Two arms	l. Unity of upaya and prajna.
m. Left leg bent and right leg extended	m. Not dwelling in extremes of samsara or nirvana.
n. Corpse seat	n. Death of ego.
o. Sun and moon: disc seats (only the sun is shown)	o. Sun: wisdom Moon: compassion.
p. Lotus seat	p. Spontaneous birth of enlightenment.
q. Vajrayogini's form: red and blazing with rays of light	q. Enraged against the hordes of maras and very wrathful. Also prajna-paramita.
Not shown:	
r. Necklace of red flowers	r. Total nonattachment.

Karma Kagyü lineage, the directness of this communication becomes apparent.

The Vajrayogini Sadhana in the Karma Kagyü Lineage

The abhisheka of Vajrayogini is an ancient ceremony which is part of the *Vajrayogini Sadhana,* the manual and liturgy of Vajrayogini practice. There are many sadhanas of Vajrayogini, including those according to Saraha, Nagarjuna, Luyipa, Jalandhara, and Savari. In the Karma Kagyü tradition, one practices the sadhana of Vajrayogini according to the Indian *siddha* Tilopa, the forefather of the Kagyü lineage.

According to spiritual biographies, after studying the basic Buddhist teachings for many years, Tilopa (998–1069 C.E.) traveled to Uddiyana, the home of the *dakinis,* or female yidams, to seek vajrayana transmission. He gained entrance to the palace of the dakinis and received direct instruction there from Vajrayogini herself, who manifested to him as the great queen of the dakinis. It may be rather perplexing to speak of encountering Vajrayogini in anthropomorphic form, when she is discussed throughout this article as the essence of egolessness. However, this account of Tilopa's meeting is the traditional story of his encounter with the direct energy and power of Vajrayogini.

Naropa (1016–1100), who received the oral transmission of the Vajrayogini practice from Tilopa, was a great scholar at Nalanda University. Following a visit from a dakini who appeared to him as an ugly old hag, he realized that he had not grasped the inner meaning of the teachings, and he set out to find his guru. After encountering many obstacles, Naropa found Tilopa dressed in beggar's rags, eating fish heads by the side of a lake. In spite of this external appearance, Naropa at once recognized his guru. He remained with him for many years and underwent numerous trials before receiving final empowerment as the holder of his lineage.

From Naropa, the oral tradition of the Vajrayogini practice passed to Marpa (1012–1097), the first Tibetan holder of the lineage. Marpa made three journeys from Tibet to India to receive instruction from Naropa. It is said that, during his third visit to India, Marpa met Vajrayogini in the form of a young maiden. With a crystal hooked knife she slashed open her belly, and Marpa saw in her belly the mandala of Vajrayogini surrounded by a spinning mantra wheel. At that moment, he had a realization of Vajrayogini as the

Coemergent Mother, a principle that will be discussed later. This realization was included in the oral transmission of Vajrayogini, which has been passed down to the present day.

Marpa gave the oral instructions for the Vajrayogini practice to the renowned *yogin* Milarepa (1040–1123); he in turn transmitted them to Gampopa (1079–1153), a great scholar and practitioner who established the monastic order of the Kagyü. Chief among Gampopa's many disciples were the founders of the "four great and eight lesser schools" of the Kagyü tradition. The Karma Kagyü, one of the four great schools, was founded by Tüsum Khyenpa (1110–1193), the first Karmapa and a foremost disciple of Gampopa. Since that time, the Karma Kagyü lineage has been headed by a succession of Karmapas, numbering sixteen in all. Tüsum Khyenpa handed down the oral transmission of the *Vajrayogini Sadhana* to Drogön Rechenpa (1088–1158); from him it was passed to Pomdrakpa, who transmitted it to the second Karmapa, Karma Pakshi (1206–1283). Karma Pakshi passed the Vajrayogini transmission to Ugyenpa (1230–1309), who gave it to Rangjung Dorje (1284–1339), the third Karmapa. It was Rangjung Dorje, the third Karmapa, who composed the written form of the sadhana of Vajrayogini according to Tilopa and the oral instructions of Marpa, which is still practiced today. It is this sadhana that is the basis for this discussion of the Vajrayogini principle.

The first Trungpa was a student of the siddha, Trungmasé (fifteenth century), who was a close disciple of the fifth Karmapa, Teshin Shekpa (1384–1415). When Naropa transmitted the teachings of Vajrayogini to Marpa, he told him that these teachings should be kept as a transmission from one teacher to one student for thirteen generations, and then they could be propagated to others. This transmission is called *chig gyü,* the "single lineage" or "single thread" transmission. Because of this, the Kagyü lineage is frequently called the *hearing lineage*. Trungmasé received the complete teachings on Vajrayogini, Chakrasamvara, and the Four-Armed Mahakala, and these became a special transmission that he was to hold. Since Trungmasé belonged to the thirteenth generation, he became the first guru to transmit this particular lineage of *mahamudra* teachings to more than a single dharma successor, and in fact he taught it widely. The first Trungpa, Künga Gyaltsen, was one of Trungmasé's disciples who received this transmission. As the eleventh Trungpa Tulku, I received the Vajrayogini transmission from Rölpé Dorjé, the regent abbot of Surmang and one of my main tutors.

Since 1970, when I arrived in America, I have been working to plant the buddhadharma, and particularly the vajra-yana teachings, in American soil. Beginning in 1977 and every year since then, those of my students who have completed the preliminary vajrayana practices, as well as extensive training in the basic meditative disciplines, have received the abhisheka of Vajrayogini. There are now (1980) more than three hundred vajrayogini *sadhakas* (practitioners of the sadhana) in our community, and there are also many Western students studying with other Tibetan teachers and practicing various vajrayana sadhanas. So the Vajrayogini abhisheka and sadhana are not purely part of Tibetan history; they have a place in the history of Buddhism in America as well.

The Ceremony of Abhisheka

The abhisheka of Vajrayogini belongs to the highest of the four orders of tantra: *anuttara tantra*. *Anuttara* means "highest," "unsurpassed," or "unequaled." Anuttara tantra can be subdivided into three parts: mother, father, and nondual.

The Karma Kagyü lineage particularly emphasizes the teachings of the mother tantra, to which Vajrayogini belongs.

Mother tantra stresses devotion as the starting point for vajrayana practice. Therefore, the key point in receiving the abhisheka is to have one-pointed devotion to the teacher. By receiving abhisheka, one is introduced to the freedom of the vajra world. In the abhisheka, the vajra master manifests as the essence of this freedom, which is the essence of Vajrayogini. He therefore represents the yidam as well as the teacher in human form. Thus, when one receives abhisheka, it is essential to understand that the yidam and the guru are not separate.

In the tradition of anuttara tantra, the student receives a fourfold abhisheka. The entire ceremony is called an abhisheka, and each of the four parts is also called an abhisheka, because each is a particular empowerment. The four abhishekas are all connected with experiencing the phenomenal world as a sacred mandala.

Before receiving the first abhisheka, the student reaffirms the refuge and bodhisattva vows. At this point the attitude of the student must be one of loving-kindness for all beings, with a sincere desire to benefit others. The student then takes a vow called the samaya vow, which binds the teacher, the student, and the yidam together. As part of this oath, the student vows that he or she will not reveal his or her vajrayana experience to others who are not included in the mandala of Vajrayogini. The student then drinks what is known as the samaya oath water from a conch shell on the shrine, to seal this vow. It is said that if the student violates this oath the water will become molten iron: it will burn the student from within and she will die on the spot. On the other hand, if the student keeps his vow and discipline, the oath water will act to propagate the student's sanity and experience of the glory, brilliance, and dignity of the vajra world. The notion of samaya will be discussed in greater detail after the discussions of the abhisheka itself.

After taking the samaya oath, the student receives the first abhisheka, the abhisheka of the vase (kalasha abhisheka), also known as the *water abhisheka*. Symbolically, the abhisheka of the vase is the coronation of the student as a prince or princess—a would-be king or queen of the mandala. It signifies the student's graduation from the ordinary world into the world of continuity, the tantric world.

The abhisheka of the vase has five parts, each of which is also called an abhisheka. In the first part, which is also called the *abhisheka of the vase,* the student is given water to drink from a vase on the shrine, called the *tsobum.* The tsobum is the principal abhisheka vase and is used to empower the student. The text of the abhisheka says:

> Just as when the Buddha was born
> The devas bathed him,
> Just so with pure, divine water
> We are empowered.

Receiving the water from the tsobum in the first abhisheka of the vase symbolizes psychological cleansing as well as empowerment. Before ascending the throne, the young prince or princess must bathe and put on fresh clothes. The five abhishekas of the vase are connected with the five buddha families. The first abhisheka of the vase is connected with the vajra family; the student is presented with a five-pointed vajra scepter, symbolizing his ability to transmute aggression into mirror-like wisdom.

In the second abhisheka of the vase, the *crown abhisheka,* the student is presented with a crown inlaid with five jewels representing the wisdom of the five buddha families. He is symbolically crowned as a confident and accomplished student worthy of taking his place in the mandala of Vajrayogini. The crown abhisheka is connected with the ratna family; the student is also presented with a jewel, the symbol of the ratna wisdom of equanimity. There is a sense of being enriched, a feeling of openness and generosity, and a sense of confidence that one is able to overcome any sense of threat or poverty.

In the third abhisheka of the vase, the *abhisheka of the vajra,* the student is presented with a nine-pronged vajra scepter, or *dorjé.* The vajra is the symbol of indestructibility and of complete skillfulness in working with the phenomenal world. So, in receiving the vajra the student is presented with the means to overcome obstacles and to propagate vajra sanity. The abhisheka of the vajra is related to the padma family: although the vajra is both a powerful scepter and a deadly weapon, its power comes from generating and extending compassion, warmth, and generosity. The student is also presented with a lotus, the symbol of the padma family, signifying the ability to transmute the grasping quality of desire into discriminating-awareness wisdom.

The *abhisheka of the ghanta,* or bell, is the fourth abhisheka of the vase. Presenting the student with the ghanta signifies that he is not only concerned with personal realization but is also willing to proclaim the teachings for the benefit of others. The piercing sound of the ghanta signifies that the vajra proclamation of truth is unobstructed. The abhisheka of the ghanta is connected with the karma family. The student is presented with a sword, the symbol of the karma family, signifying the wisdom of all-accomplishing action which conquers neurotic speed and jealousy.

The final abhisheka of the vase is the *abhisheka of name.* In this abhisheka, the vajra master rings a ghanta with a vajra attached to it above the student's head. When the bell rings, the student is given a tantric name, which is a secret name. This name is not publicized like an ordinary name, but when the practitioner needs to use his power to wake someone up, he says his own vajra name, his secret name, as a reminder of vajra nature. The giving of the secret name signifies the final act in the coronation of the tantric prince or princess. Because of merit accumulated through practice and devotion to the teacher, the student deserves to change his or her name from a common name to that of a would-be king or queen, a potential master of the mandala; the student is acknowledged as a future *tathagata*.

The abhisheka of name is connected with the buddha family. There is a sense of complete spaciousness and openness that comes when one takes one's place in the vajra mandala. Having been coronated, the student is presented with a hooked knife, which Vajrayogini holds in her right hand. At this point, the student is introduced to the chief deity of the mandala and to her buddhalike quality, which is the wisdom of all-encompassing space. Although Vajrayogini is red in color, symbolizing her feminine quality of warmth and passion, her basic quality is definitely that of the buddha family.

Having received the complete abhisheka of the vase, there is a sense of significant psychological progress and psychological change in the student. At that point, the vajra master is able to confer the remaining three abhishekas. We cannot go into too much detail about these aspects of the ceremony. But in brief, the second abhisheka is known as the *secret abhisheka* (*guhya abhisheka*). By drinking *amrita*—a mixture of liquor and other substances—from the skull cup on the shrine, the mind of the student merges with the mind of the teacher and the mind of the yidam, so that the boundary between confusion and wakefulness begins to dissolve. In the third abhisheka, the *prajnajnana abhisheka*, or abhisheka of knowledge and wisdom, the student begins to experience joy, *mahasukha*—a uniting with the world. This is sometimes called the *union of bliss and emptiness*, which signifies greater openness and greater vision taking place.

The fourth abhisheka (*chaturtha abhisheka*) is known as the *abhisheka of suchness*. The student experiences that he or she does not have to dwell on the past, present, or future; he could just wake himself up on the spot. The student's mind is opened into the ultimate notion of sacred outlook, in which there is nobody to "flash" sacred outlook. There is just a sense of the doer and the doing dissolving into one, which is a sense of basic shock: the possibilities of conventional mind are dissolving into nothing.

Samaya

The principle of samaya, or sacred bondage, becomes extremely important once we have taken abhisheka. The definition of yidam as the "sacred bondage of one's mind" was discussed earlier. When we receive empowerment to practice the sadhana of Vajrayogini, we take on that samaya, or bondage. We bind ourselves to indestructible wakefulness, committing ourselves fully to maintaining sacred outlook throughout our lives. This is done by identifying oneself completely with the vajra sanity of the teacher and of Vajrayogini. One is inseparably bound together with the teacher and the yidam; and, at this point, one's very being and one's sanity depend on keeping up this commitment.

This is not to say that if a student has one "bad" thought or trace of confusion he will be rejected or destroyed. There is still a sense of journey and path that takes place once one has received abhisheka. In fact, it is said that samaya is nearly impossible to keep: it is like a mirror in that, no matter how thoroughly it is polished, it always collects dust and must be polished again. In taking abhisheka, one is taught to experience sacred outlook on the spot, which *is* samaya. When obstacles or difficulties arise, they become reminders of sacred outlook rather than purely hindrances. This is called the samaya of experiencing everything as sacred in vajra nature, which has three categories: the samaya of body, or mudra; the samaya of speech, or mantra; the samaya of mind, or vajra.

The samaya of body involves always regarding one's basic phenomenal situation as an expression of sacredness. We do not doubt the sacredness of our world. The samaya of speech involves also regarding any occurrence—anything that comes up in our experience—as sacred. This could be either an internal or an external occurrence, so that any subconscious gossip or emotional upheaval is included here. The samaya of mind is connected with the indestructible wakefulness of the vajra mandala—in this case the mandala of Vajrayogini. Even the hint or the possibility of neurosis is unable to enter into one's state of being because the whole world is seen as part of the mandala of sacredness that one has entered.

It is interesting that abhisheka brings both a greater sense of freedom and a greater sense of bondage. The more we develop a sense of openness, of letting go and shedding ego, the more we develop a commitment to the world of sanity. So taking abhisheka and beginning yidam practice is a very serious step. In fact, we should be somewhat frightened of it and, at the same time, we could appreciate it as the most precious opportunity to realize our human birth.

Coemergent Wisdom

Fundamentally, the magic of the vajrayana tradition is the ability to transform confusion into wisdom on the spot. From the point of view of vajrayana, real magic, or *siddhi* in Sanskrit, is the ability to work with and tame one's mind. This is completely different from the usual notion of magic as a supernatural power over the universe. As mentioned in the previous discussion of the samayas of body, speech, and mind, any potential confusion and neurosis becomes an opportunity to experience sacred outlook. At the beginning of the path of meditation, we work to tame our minds and subdue the forces of confusion. In the mahayana, we see the emptiness of self and phenomena; out of that, we rouse compassion for beings who do not realize the emptiness, and therefore the freedom, of their nature. In the vajrayana, we could actually bring together confusion and enlightenment on one spot, and thereby completely overcome the dualism of samsara and nirvana.

The simultaneous experience of confusion and sanity, or being asleep and awake, is the realization of *coemergent wisdom*. Any occurrence in one's state of mind—any thought, feeling, or emotion—is both black and white; it is both a statement of confusion and a message of enlightened mind. Confusion is seen so clearly that this clarity itself *is* sacred outlook. Vajrayogini is called "the Coemergent Mother." In fact, the sadhana of Vajrayogini according to Tilopa is entitled *The Sadhana of the Glorious Coemergent Mother Vajrayogini*. By practicing the sadhana and by identifying ourselves with the body, speech, and mind of the yidam, we become able to experience the coemergent boundary between confusion and wakefulness. Then we can use confusion itself as a steppingstone for realizing further sanity and further wisdom.

Visualization

A practitioner's connection to, and understanding of, the iconography come about through the visualization practice of Vajrayogini. There are two stages of visualization practice: *utpattikrama* (*kyerim* in Tibetan) and *sampannakrama* (*dzogrim* in Tibetan). *Utpattikrama* literally means "developing stage," and *sampannakrama* means "fulfillment stage." Utpattikrama is the process of visualizing the yidam, in this case, Vajrayogini. In the self-visualization, the practitioner visualizes himself as the yidam. The visualization arises from shunyata, or emptiness, as do all tantric visualizations. The text amplifies this concept:

> All the dharmas comprising grasping and fixation become empty. From within emptiness . . . arises the triangular source of dharmas . . . On that is the nature of my consciousness . . . Like a fish leaping from water, I arise in the body of Jetsun Vajrayogini.

So the process of visualizing oneself as the yidam comes first from the experience of emptiness and egolessness. Out of that arises the source of dharmas, the abstract form of coemergence; and on that, the practitioner visualizes himself as the yidam. The visualization, therefore, is essentially empty as well. The practice of visualization is identifying oneself with the yidam, realizing the deity as the nonmanifested, or empty, manifestation of basic enlightened nature. The form of the yidam, including her clothing, ornaments, and stance, represents aspects of the enlightened state of mind. So when one visualizes oneself as a blazing, youthful red lady decked with bone ornaments, one is not particularly trying to conjure up an exotic costume as the latest fashion, but one is identifying oneself as Vajrayogini as the embodiment of wisdom and compassion.

The visualization of oneself as Vajrayogini is called the *samayasattva:* the "sacred bondage of one's being." The samayasattva is basically the expression of the samayas of body, speech, and mind. It expresses one's commitment to the teacher and the teachings and one's trust in one's fundamental state of mind.

Having visualized the samayasattvas of basic being, one invites what is known as *jnanasattva*. The jnanasattva is another level of being or experience. Jnana is a state of wakefulness or openness, whereas samaya is an experience of bondage, of being solidly grounded in one's experience. *Jnana* literally means "wisdom" or, more accurately, "being wise." One invites this state of wisdom, this level of wakefulness, into one's own imperfect visualization, so that the visualization comes alive with a feeling of openness and humor.

At the conclusion of the visualization practice, the visualization is dissolved back into the emptiness and one meditates, or rests, in that nondual state of mind. This is the sampannakrama, or fulfillment, stage. It is said in the tantric texts that the proper understanding of visualization practice is that the utpattikrama and sampannakrama stages are not fundamentally different; that is, in this case, the sampannakrama experience of emptiness-emptiness and the utpattikrama experience of form-emptiness should not be seen as two things, but as one expression of the world of the Coemergent Mother.

Sampannakrama meditation is similar to the practice of shamatha-vipashyana; in fact, without prior training in these meditation practices, it is impossible to practice sampannakrama. Sampannakrama is an expression of vastness. Experiencing the vajra mind of Vajrayogini is so deep and vast that if thoughts arise, they do not become highlights: they are small fish in a huge ocean of space.

The Vajrayogini Principle and Its Iconography

An examination of the meaning of the following praise to Vajrayogini from the sadhana may help us to understand the

Vajrayogini principle in relation to the iconography of
Vajrayogini. The praise begins:

> Bhagavati Vajrayogini,
> Personification of vajra emptiness,
> Blazing with the kalpa-ending fire, uttering
>   the terrifying sound of HUM—
> We prostrate to Vajra-chandali.

Bhagavati means "blessed one." This stanza refers first to
Vajrayogini as the anthropomorphic form of shunyata, the
"personification of vajra emptiness." It then praises her fiery
quality of passion and cosmic lust. In the iconography,
Vajrayogini's body is red and blazes with rays of light, which
is described here as "blazing with the kalpa-ending fire."
This is her padma family quality, which transmutes neurotic
passion into all-consuming compassion. *Kalpa* means "a historical era." The "kalpa-ending fire" in Indian mythology is
an explosion of the sun, which burns up the solar system
and brings an end to the kalpa. Vajrayogini's passion is so
bright and so consuming that it is likened to that fire. The
"terrifying sound of HUM" expresses the wrath of her passion, which is terrifying to ego. *Chandali* (*tummo* in Tibetan)
is the yogic heat, cosmic heat, in yogic practice, which is
again the Vajrayogini principle of passion arising free from
habitual tendencies. Such passion is immensely powerful; it
radiates its warmth in all directions. It simultaneously nur-
tures the welfare of beings and blazes to destroy the neurotic
tendencies of ego. The praise continues:

> Your sow's face manifesting nonthought,
>   the unchanging dharmakaya,
> You benefit beings with wrathful mercy;
> Accomplishing their welfare; with horrific
>   accoutrements.
> We prostrate to you who benefit beings in
>   nonthought.

Nonthought is an important aspect of the Vajrayogini principle. It is the experience of mind totally freed from the habitual chatter of ego, freed from the grasping and fixation that give rise to neurotic thought patterns. Until the aggression and wildness of mind are tamed through meditation practice, there is no possibility of experiencing the nonthought possibilities in one's mind.

Vajrayogini is often depicted with a sow's head over her right ear. When she wears this ornament, she is referred to as Vajravarahi, "Vajra Sow." The sow traditionally represents ignorance or stupidity. In this case, the sow's head symbolizes the transmutation of ignorance, or delusion, into the vajra ignorance, which is nonthought or complete spaciousness of mind.

This stanza equates nonthought with *dharmakaya*, which, roughly translated, is the primordial mind of buddha. The practice of the *Vajrayogini Sadhana* is very much connected with realizing this primordial non–reference point. The purpose of the sadhana practice is not so much to cut immediate thoughts as it is to cut the habitual tendencies that are the root of discursive thought.

The "horrific accoutrements" referred to in the stanza are the necklace of freshly severed heads that Vajrayogini wears. It says in the sadhana that she wears this necklace because "the fifty-one samskaras are completely purified." *Samskara* means "formations," which refers to concepts. Vajrayogini's necklace of heads signifies that all habitual concepts are purified or destroyed in nonthought.

The praise continues:

> Terrifying heroine who annihilates the unsuitable,
> With three eyes, clenched fangs, the absolute
>   trikaya,
> Your terrifying cry cuts off the kleshas.
> We prostrate to you who subjugate and conquer
>   the maras.

Vajrayogini is frequently called the conqueror of the *maras*, which are the forces of woldly confusion. In the stories of the Buddha's enlightenment, Mara, "the Evil One," sends his daughters, the four maras, to tempt Shakyamuni and his armies to attack him. Vanquishing them, Shakyamuni becomes the Buddha, "the Awakened One." Thus, the basic idea of Vajrayogini as the conqueror of the maras is the conquest of ego. From ego's point of view, Vajrayogini is "terrifying" because her wakefulness is so piercing and uncompromising. At another point the sadhana says: "Grimacing wrathfully to subdue the four maras, she clenches her fangs and bites her lower lip." This further explains the stanza's reference to Vajrayogini's fierceness.

The reference to Vajrayogini's three eyes means that nothing escapes the vision of Vajrayogini; therefore, ego has nowhere to hide. The sadhana also says: "Because she is the knower of the past, present, and future, she rolls her three furious bloodshot eyes."

The notion that Vajrayogini is "the absolute *trikaya*" is that her wisdom and skillful means manifest on all levels of body and mind: the *dharmakaya* level of absolute, primordial mind; the *sambhogakaya* level of energy, emotions, and symbols; and the *nirmanakaya* level of manifested form, or body. The trikaya also refers to the levels of body, speech, and mind in one's practice, which are the levels of physical body, the emotions and concepts, and the basic spaciousness of mind. Vajrayogini joins all of those levels together, and again she leaves no place for the maras to hide.

The stanza also says that her terrifying cry "cuts off the kleshas." *Kleshas*, or obscurations, refer to conflicting emotions, neurotic emotion. The five kleshas are passion, aggression, delusion, jealousy, and pride, all of which are subjugated by the Vajrayogini principle.

The next stanza reads:

Naked, with loosed hair, of faultless and terrifying
form;
Beyond the vice of the kleshas, benefiting sentient
beings;
You lead beings from the six realms with your
hook of mercy.
We prostrate to you who accomplish Buddha
activity.

Vajrayogini is naked because she is completely untouched
by the neurosis of the kleshas; therefore she has no armor of
ego to clothe her. Because of this, she is able to "do benefit
for sentient beings," to extend absolute compassion to them.
The reference to her loosed hair signifies her compassion for
beings. The "hook of mercy" refers to Vajrayogini's hooked
knife, with which she lifts beings out of the suffering of the
six realms, or samsara, into the vajra world. Therefore, she
completely accomplishes action that is free from karmic de-
filement—*buddha activity*, or action that is completely
awake.

The next stanza reads:

Dwelling in the charnel ground, subjugating
Rudra and his wife,
Wrathful, fearsome, uttering the sound of PHAT,
You benefit beings with the mercy of your skill.
We prostrate to the wrathful one who subjugates
the maras.

The "charnel ground" refers to the basic space in which
birth and death, confusion and wakefulness arise—the
ground of coemergence. Vajrayogini is not an ethereal principle; she dwells in the heart of samsaric chaos, which is also
the heart of wisdom. "Rudra and his wife" refers to ego and
its embellishments, which Vajrayogini subjugates utterly.

She is "the terrifying heroine who annihilates the unsuitable"; therefore, "she is wrathful and fearsome and utters the sound of PHAT," a syllable associated with subjugation, destruction of ego-clinging, and the proclamation of vajra truth. At the same time, she is skilled and merciful. Combining these qualities, she is, again, the subjugator of the maras.

The next verse reads:

> You have realized ultimate dharmata and
>   abandoned death.
> On a seat of a corpse, sun, moon, and lotus,
> Your wrathful form is beautified with all the
>   ornaments.
> We prostrate to you who have perfected all good
>   qualities.

The lotus, sun disk, and moon disk are the customary seats for both buddhas and yidams in tantric iconography. The lotus is a symbol of purity, and it also signifies the birth of enlightenment amidst the world of confused existence. The sun symbolizes jnana, or wisdom, while the moon is a symbol of bodhichitta, or compassion. The fact that Vajrayogini also stands on a corpse signifies that she is a semiwrathful deity. There are peaceful, semiwrathful, and wrathful yidams in tantric iconography. The peaceful deities represent the energy of pacifying and taming while semiwrathful and wrathful yidams work more directly and forcefully with passion, aggression, and delusion—conquering and trampling them on the spot.

The figure of the corpse symbolizes the death of ego and shows that Vajrayogini has "abandoned death." "Ultimate dharmata" in the stanza is a reference to Vajrayogini's stance. In an earlier section of the sadhana, it says: "Since she does not dwell in the extremes of samsara or nirvana, she stands on a seat of a lotus, corpse, and sun-disk, with her left leg bent and her right leg raised in dancing posture." The idea of ultimate *dharmata* is transcending the dualism, or extremes, of samsara and nirvana by realizing coemergent wisdom: seeing how confusion and enlightenment arise simultaneously. *Dharmata* means "the state of dharma." It is complete realization of the dharma, which is seeing the "isness" or "suchness" of reality.

This stanza also refers to the ornaments that beautify Vajrayogini's wrathful form: her bone headdress, her bone earrings, her necklace, her girdle, and her anklets and bracelets. These present her perfection of generosity, discipline, patience, exertion, and meditation—five of the six *paramitas*, or transcendent actions of the mahayana. The perfection of the sixth paramita, prajna, is not represented as an ornament because the being of Vajrayogini is itself the epitome of prajna. Thus she is called Prajnaparamita. Prajna as the perception of shunyata was mentioned earlier. At the level of prajnaparamita, prajna is complete, nondual realization which cuts through any clinging to either existence or nonexistence. Prajnaparamita is also called "the Mother of All the Buddhas": all the buddhas of the past, present, and future are born from this stainless good knowledge which shows the nature of phenomena as shunyata. In an earlier section of the sadhana, Vajrayogini is praised as Prajnaparamita:

> Prajnaparamita, inexpressible by speech or
> thought,
> Unborn, unceasing, with a nature like sky,
> Only experienced by discriminating awareness
> wisdom,
> Mother of the victorious ones of the three times,
> we praise you and prostrate.

The next stanza reads:

> Holding a hooked-knife, skull cup, and khatvanga
> in your hands,
> Possessing the light of wisdom, cutting off the
> kleshas.
> As the spontaneous trikaya, you cut off the three
> poisons.
> We prostrate to you who benefit beings.

The second line—"Possessing the light of wisdom, cutting off the kleshas"—further emphasizes the Vajrayogini principle as Prajnaparamita, the essence of discriminating-awareness wisdom.

The hooked knife has been discussed as Vajrayogini's "hook of mercy." It is also a weapon that is used to slice through the deceptions of ego. It is a symbol of the power and cutting quality of nonthought. In her left hand Vajrayogini holds a skull cup, or *kapala*, filled with amrita, representing the principle of intoxicating extreme beliefs. The kapala filled with amrita is also a symbol of wisdom. The *khatvanga* is the staff that Vajrayogini holds up against her shoulders. It represents her skillful means. The staff is also the secret symbol of Vajrayogini's union with her consort, Chakrasamvara, who is the essence of skillful means.

On the kharvanga are three heads representing the trikaya principle mentioned in this stanza. The reference to Vajrayogini as the spontaneous trikaya means that the brilliance of her wisdom applies equally to all levels of experience. Because of the universality of her wisdom, she utterly cuts off the three poisons: passion, aggression, and delusion. In doing so, she benefits beings.

The next stanza reads:

> Self-born great bliss, O Vajrayogini,
> Unchanging wisdom vajra of dharmakaya,

Nonthought, unconditioned wisdom, absolute
dharmadhatu—
We prostrate to your pure, nondual form.

Again, this stanza praises Vajrayogini as the essence of wisdom, which is the primordial "wisdom vajra of dharmakaya" and the even more primordial "unconditioned wisdom" of "absolute dharmadhatu"; this wisdom is completely nondual. Beyond that, this stanza brings together the Vajrayogini principle of wisdom with the principle of the great bliss, mahasukha, which is self-born, that is, self-existing rather than created or manufactured by conceptual mind.

Mahasukha is an actual experience of bliss—a physical, psychological, total experience of joy that comes from being completely without discursive thoughts, completely in the realm of nonthought. One unites with the nondual, awake state of being. This experience is the fruition of the Vajrayogini practice; it comes only from complete identification with the wisdom mind of the yidam. According to the scriptures, mahasukha and wisdom are indivisible; therefore, the practice of Vajrayogini leads to this experience of the self-born great bliss because she is the essence of wisdom.

In the next stanza of the praise, the third line reads:

Self-born great bliss, you are ultimate mahamudra

This refers to Vajrayogini. Experiencing mahasukha, or the wisdom of bliss and emptiness, is the realization of *mahamudra*, which is the pinnacle of the tradition of anuttara tantra. *Maha* means "great" and *mudra* means "sign" or "gesture." To experience mahamudra is to realize that the literal truth, the symbolic truth, and the absolute truth are actually one thing, that they take place on one dot, one spot. One experiences reality as the great symbol which stands for itself.

The bliss of mahamudra is not so much great pleasure,

but it is the experience of tremendous spaciousness, freedom from imprisonment, which come from seeing through the duality of existence and realizing that the essence of truth, the essence of space, is available on this very spot. The freedom of mahamudra is measureless, unspeakable, fathomless. Such fathomless space and complete freedom produce tremendous joy. This type of joy is not conditioned by even the experience of freedom itself; it is self-born, innate.

Conclusion

Some of what has been discussed here may be very difficult to grasp. In fact, it should be that way. If it were possible to experience the vajrayana simply by reading about it, it would cease to exist, because no one would practice it; everyone would simply study the texts. Luckily this does not work. The only way to gain the vajra freedom is to practice buddhadharma as it was taught by the Buddha and as it has been preserved and passed down for twenty-five hundred years.

I am very happy that it has been possible to discuss the vajrayana and the Vajrayogini tradition so genuinely and thoroughly. But the most important thing that one can ever do for oneself and others is to sit down and unravel the confusion in one's mind. This is a very, very simple thing to do, and because it is so simple, it is also very easy not to see this possibility.

It is my hope that this discussion will provide a glimpse of the vajrayana world—its grandeur and its sacredness. Sacred possibilities always exist in our lives. The goodness and the gentleness of the world are always there for us to appreciate. This is not a myth; it is actual fact. We could experience Vajrayogini at any time if we have the courage to acknowledge our own wakeful nature and the greatness of our heritage as human beings.

> Eternally brilliant, utterly empty,
> Vajra dancer, mother of all,
> I bow to you.
> The essence of all sentient beings lives as
>   Vajrayogini.
> From the milk ocean of her blessing
> Good butter is churned
> Which worthy ones receive as glory.
> May everyone eternally enjoy
> The lotus garden of the Coemergent Mother.

PART THREE

Working with Others

8

Relationship

"The idea of relationship needs to fall apart. When we realize that life is the expression of death and death is the expression of life, that continuity cannot exist without discontinuity, then there is no longer any need to cling to one and fear the other. There is no longer any ground for the brave or the cowardly. One sees that relationship is the lack of any viewpoint whatsoever."

View Based on Hope for Eternity

Eternity is one of the notions we cherish as an encouragement in our lives. We feel that since there is eternity there will be eternal communication. Somehow or other there will be an endless continuity to give meaning to things: a spiritual background or an atmosphere of transcendental promise.

We hardly realize how this attitude influences our approach toward relationships. When we become good friends with somebody in high school, we automatically expect the friendship to go on forever. It may be fifteen years since we built a cabin with a friend but now we continue to celebrate our comradeship by going over how skillfully we did the framing, the joints, what nails we used, and so on.

Composed during 1972 retreat in Charlemont, Massachusetts.

Many relationships are formed on the basis of some common pain or some shared task. We tend to make a big deal of this pain or task: we make it the keepsake of the relationship. Or else we meet someone in circumstances of lively common interest where communication flows without obstacles and then we celebrate the smoothness as if fending off a common enemy. Either way, the pain or the smoothness develops a legendary quality in regard to the relationship.

"Good friends" implies forever. You expect that the person you are committed to in that way will pour honey on your grave; otherwise you will feel you have been cheated. You are constantly struggling to keep your eternal friendship beautiful, which becomes an enormous strain on the relationship. Nevertheless, this is the model of relationship presented by theistic traditions, such as Christianity or Hinduism. Having such a relationship is regarded as behaving as God commanded or as coming closer to the example of God's own love, which is eternal.

The idea of eternity has been misunderstood; it has been used to prove the profundity of our relationship, our deathless friendship. We tend to assume that something is going to go on forever, and therefore we venerate it like someone might venerate a piece of rusty fence wire known to have been hanging on a fence at a famous Civil War battle. We venerate it for its eternity rather than for its profundity. Ironically, it actually becomes a profound statement because of the basic truth of impermanence.

In societies influenced—at the sophisticated level at least— by a nontheistic point of view, such as Buddhist or Confucian, relationship is more a matter of manners and integrity than of approaching an eternal divine model. There is less sense of guilt, but there is still a sense of righteousness or of acting justly. In the humanistic context, relationship seems to be based on a model derived from ancient patterns of barter. In the commerce of barter more is involved than just vying for monetary units: something of value has to be given and something of value has to be received in exchange. But this approach is still based on the backdrop of eternity and on the veneration of ancient models of relationship.

View Based on Fear of Death

Distrust and suspicion of eternity arise when we develop a sense of what might go wrong with the relationship—or what might go right for that matter—independent of our will. There is a suggestion of inevitable chaos or death. Fearing the independent, spontaneous development of the relationship we try to ignore our actual emotions and independent will. Brave people do this semiconsciously by developing a sense of mission or dogma in the relationship. Cowardly people manage it as a subconscious twist.

In general the brave strategy is less successful than the cowardly in creating an "ideal" relationship. This dogmatic approach can only succeed by continually making a basically illogical position logically believable to the friend or partner. Then constant maintenance of the magnificent edifice is required. The less brave but more diligent do the whole work without ever confronting the partner on major issues. Instead he or she continually puts off the sense of death onto a thousand small things. The partner forgets to put the cap back on the ketchup bottle, or always squeezes the toothpaste tube at the wrong end. The fault lies in all these little things.

In spite of philosophical and religious beliefs in eternity, there is a sense of the constant threat of death, that ultimately the relationship is doomed. Whether cowardly or brave, we are trapped in that actual situation, making a constant patchwork in order to survive.

Beyond Hope and Fear

Making a big deal out of relationship is deathly—as when in chopping an onion, we become more conscious of the chopper than the chopping process. Quite possibly we might chop our fingers off. When we begin to realize this, the sense of helplessness is startling. Viewpoint and attitude don't help. They are no more than a shell. The theistic view of naive belief in eternity and the humanistic view of good manners and dignity are both merely conventional games remote from the actuality of the situation. Their adages of relationship, such as "patience is virtue" or "death before dishonor" are not just the products of convention; they are in themselves purely conventional.

The idea of relationship needs to fall apart. When we realize that life is the expression of death and death is the expression of life, that continuity cannot exist without discontinuity, then there is no longer any need to cling to one and fear the other. There is no longer any ground for the brave or the cowardly. One sees that relationship is the lack of any viewpoint whatsoever.

We might think that such a relationship is only for the spiritually advanced, but actually it is just normal and ordinary. Any conceptual reference point becomes destructive. We actually begin to suspect that the relationship does not exist. But there is no need to worry: that nonexistence continues as a powerful breeding ground of further relationship. Such wariness is still a viewpoint, but it is one that is open to surprises, unlike living in the promise of eternity. It is also unlike complete mistrust, which does not allow the naiveté of relationship to flower. Whereas a covenant of trust breeds further mistrust, wariness of trust can bring enormously warm and genuine relationships.

9

Acknowledging Death

"We do not have to conceal the unspeakable; on the other hand, we do not have to push it to the extreme. At the least, we should help a person to have some understanding of the idea of loss—of the possibility of nonexistence and of dissolving into the unknown. The whole point of any relationship is to share some degree of honesty and to explore how far we can go with it. In that way relationships can become extremely powerful and intense, and beautiful."

In discussing sickness, whether physical or mental, we should recognize the importance of our sense of survival. We want to survive, and when we talk about healing, we are talking about how to survive. Viewed from another angle, our strategy of survival is the pattern of our reaction to the fact of death.

One's attitude toward death is central to any healing process. Although it is frequently ignored it is always in the background. No one actually wants to face the possibility of death, or even the idea of death. Even a mild sickness points to the possibility of nothingness: we might lose control of our physical or mental situation; we might become lost in mid-air. Since as healers we are dealing constantly with the

Based on 1973 seminar, "The Meaning of Death," Barnet, Vermont.

fear of loss, we should actually bring that possibility into the picture. Facing it will not exactly solve the problem, but, to begin with, the problem should at least be faced.

Many people are confused in their attitude toward death and toward dying persons: should we try to conceal the situation or should we talk about it? Sometimes we do not want to talk about what is happening because it seems that to do so would be to suggest that something is basically wrong. Because of such attitudes there is often a loss of spirit on the part of both the patient and the physician. But when we are willing to acknowledge what is really happening, we pick up spirit, or buoyancy. One could even go so far as to say that by such acknowledgment some kind of sanity develops. So I think it is very important to present the possibility to people that they might have to face some kind of loss, some sense of bewilderment. In fact, the vanguard of death is uncertainty and complete bewilderment. It would be much healthier and more helpful to relate directly to this possibility, rather than just ignoring it. The healer should encourage people who are sick to confront their uncertainty. Such open communication will allow a real meeting to take place, an honest relationship.

We do not have to try to conceal the unspeakable; on the other hand, we do not have to push it to the extreme. At the least, we should help a person to have some understanding of the idea of loss—of the possibility of nonexistence and of dissolving into the unknown. The whole point of any relationship is to share some degree of honesty and to explore how far we can go with it. In that way relationships can become extremely powerful and intense, and beautiful. Sometimes we might only be able to get a hint of this intensity; we might only open up to just the bare minimum. Still, even then it is worthwhile. It is a step in the right direction.

In the healer-patient relationship, we are not concerned

with trying to change people, particularly. Sickness and health are not black-and-white situations, but are part of an organic process. We are simply working with sickness and the potential of death, rather than relying on any particular doctrine. We are not talking about converting people. Nevertheless, the materials we have to work with are very rich; as we go along we can see the seed changing into a flower. We do not really change people; they simply grow. Encouraging patients to accept death or uncertainty does not mean that they have to face the devil. Instead such acceptance is something positive in people's lives; conquering the final fear of the unknown is very powerful.

Some people talk about healing in a magical sense, as when so-called healers put their hands on a sick person and miraculously heal them; others talk about the physical approach to healing, using drugs, surgery, and so forth. But I think the important point is that any real healing has to come out of some kind of psychological openness. There are constant opportunities for such openness—constant gaps in our conceptual and physical structures. If we begin to breathe out, then we create room for fresh air to rush in. If we do not breathe, there is no way for the fresh air to enter. It is a question of psychological attitude rather than of being taken over by external powers that heal us. Openness seems to be the only key to healing. And openness means we are willing to acknowledge that we are worthy; we have some kind of ground to relate with whatever is happening to us.

The role of the healer is not just to cure the disease; it is to cut through the tendency to see disease as an external threat. By providing companionship and some kind of sympathy, the healer creates a suggestion of health or underlying sanity, which then undermines naive conceptions of disease. The healer deals with the mishandling of the gaps that occur in one's life, with one's losses of spirit.

People tend to feel that their particular sickness is something special, that they are the only person with such an illness. But in fact, their illness is not so special—nor so terrible. It is a question of acknowledging that we are born alone and that we die alone, but that it is still okay. There is nothing particularly terrible or special about it.

Often the whole notion of sickness is taken as a purely mechanical problem: something is wrong with one's machine, one's body. But somehow that is missing the point. It is not the sickness that is the big problem, but the psychological state behind it. We could not have gotten sick in the first place without some kind of loss of interest and attention. Whether we were run down by a car or we caught a cold, there was some gap in which we did not take care of ourselves—an empty moment in which we ceased to relate to things properly. There was no ongoing awareness of our psychological state. So to the extent that we invite it to begin with, all sicknesses—and not just those diseases traditionally considered to be psychosomatic—are psychological. All diseases are instigated by one's state of mind. And even after we have dealt with the disease and the symptoms have disappeared, by pretending that the problem is over we only plant seeds for further neurosis.

It seems that we generally avoid our psychological responsibility, as though diseases were external events imposing themselves upon us. There is a quality of sleepiness, and of missing the gaps in the seemingly solid structure of our lives. Out of that sense of carelessness comes an immense message. Our bodies demand our attention; our bodies demand that we actually pay attention to what is going on with our lives. Illness brings us down to earth, making things seem much more direct and immediate.

Disease is a direct message to develop a proper attitude of mindfulness: we should be more intelligent about ourselves.

Our minds and bodies are both very immediate. You alone know how your body feels. No one else cares; no one else can know but you. So there is a natural wakefulness about what is good for you and what is not. You can respond intelligently to your body by paying attention to your state of mind.

Because of this the practice of meditation may be the only way to really cure ourselves. Although the attempt to use meditation as some sort of cure may seem materialistic, the practice itself soon cuts through any materialistic attitude. Basically, mindfulness is a sense of composure. In meditation we are not accomplishing anything; we are just there, seeing our lives. There is a general sense of watchfulness, and an awareness of the body as an extremely sensitive mechanism which gives us messages constantly. If we have missed all the rest of the opportunities to relate with these messages, we find ourselves sick. Our bodies force us to be mindful on the spot. So it is important not to try to get rid of the sickness but to use it as a message.

We view our desire to get rid of disease as a desire to live. But instead it is often just the opposite: it is an attempt to avoid life. Although we seemingly want to be alive, in fact we simply want to avoid intensity. It is an ironic twist: we actually want to be healed in order to avoid life. So the hope for cure is a big lie; it is the biggest conspiracy of all. In fact, all entertainment—whether it is the movies or various programs for so-called self-growth—lures us into feeling that we are in touch with life, while in fact we are putting ourselves into a further stupor.

The healing relationship is a meeting of two minds: that of the healer and patient, or for that matter, of the spiritual teacher and student. If you and the other person are both open, some kind of dialogue can take place that is not forced. Communication occurs naturally because both are in the same situation. If the patient feels terrible, the healer picks up that sense of the patient's wretchedness: for a moment he feels more or less the same, as if he himself were sick. For a moment the two are not separate and a sense of authenticity takes place. From the patient's point of view, that is precisely what is needed: someone acknowledges his existence and the fact that he needs help very badly. Someone actually sees through his sickness. The healing process can then begin to take place in the patient's state of being, because he realizes that someone has communicated with him completely. There has been a mutual glimpse of common ground. The psychological underpinning of the sickness then begins to come apart, to dissolve. The same thing applies to meetings between a meditation teacher and his or her student. There is a flash of understanding—nothing particularly mystical or "far out," as they say—just very simple, direct communication. The student understands and the teacher understands at the same moment. In this common flash of understanding, knowledge is imparted.

At this point I am not making any distinction between physicians and psychiatrists: whether we are dealing at the psychological or the medical level, the relationship with one's patient has to be exactly the same. The atmosphere of acceptance is extremely simple but very effective. The main point is that the healer and the patient are able to share their sense of pain and suffering—their claustrophobia or fear or physical pain. The healer has to feel herself to be part of that whole setup. It seems that many healers avoid that kind of identification; they do not want to get involved in such an intense experience. Instead they try to play extremely cool and unconcerned, taking a more businesslike approach.

We all speak the same language; we experience a similar type of birth and a similar exposure to death. So there is bound to always be some link, some continuity between you and the other. It is something more than just mechanically saying "Yes, I know; it hurts very badly." Rather than just sympathizing with the patient, it is important to actually feel her pain and share her anxiety. You can then say "Yes, I feel that pain" in a different way. To relate with total openness means that you are completely captured by someone's problem. There may be a sense of not knowing quite how to handle it and just having to do your best, but even such clumsiness is an enormously generous statement. So, complete openness and bewilderment meet at a very fine point.

There is much more involved in the healer-patient relationship than just going by the books and looking up the appropriate medicine. According to Buddhism, the human essence is compassion and wisdom. So you do not have to acquire skillful communication from outside yourself; you have it already. It has nothing to do with mystical experience or any kind of higher spiritual ecstasy; it is just the basic working situation. If you have an interest in something, that is openness. If you have an interest in people's suffering and conflicts, you have that openness constantly. And then you can develop some sense of trust and understanding, so that your openness becomes compassion.

It is possible to work with sixty people a day and have something click with each of them. It requires a sense of complete dedication, and a willingness to stay alert, without trying to achieve a specific goal. If you have a goal, then you are trying to manipulate the interaction and healing cannot take place. You need to understand your patients and encourage them to communicate, but you cannot force them. Only then can the patient, who is feeling a sense of separation, which is also a sense of death, begin to feel that there is hope. At last someone really cares for him, someone really does listen, even if it is only for a few seconds. That allows intense, very genuine communication to take place. Such communication is simple: there is no trick behind it and no complicated tradition to learn. It is not a question of learning *how* to do it, but of just going ahead with it.

Psychiatrists and physicians, as well as their patients, have to come to terms with their sense of anxiety about the possibility of nonexistence. When there is that kind of openness, the healer does not have to solve a person's problem completely. The approach of trying to repair everything has always been a problem in the past; such an approach creates a successive string of cures and deceptions, which seem to go hand in hand. Once the basic fear is acknowledged, continuing with the treatment becomes very easy. The path comes to you: there is no need to try to create the path for yourself. Healing professionals have the advantage of being able to develop themselves by working with the great variety of situations that come to them. There are endless possibilities for developing one's awareness and openness. Of course, it is always easier to look down on your patients and their predicament, thinking how lucky you are that you do not have their diseases. You can feel somewhat superior. But the acknowledgment of your common ground—your common experience of birth, old age, sickness, and death, and the fear that underlies all of those—brings a sense of humility. That is the beginning of the healing process. The rest seems to follow quite easily and naturally, based on one's inherent wisdom and compassion. This is not a particularly mystical or spiritual process; it is simple, ordinary human experience. The first time you try to approach a person in this way it may seem to be difficult. But you just do it on the spot.

And finally, what do we mean when we say that a patient has been healed? To be healed, ironically, means that a person is no longer embarrassed by life; she is able to face death without resentment or expectation.

Alcohol as Medicine or Poison

"In the Guhyasamaja Tantra, the Buddha says, "That which intoxicates the dualistic mind is the natural antideath potion indeed." In the Buddhist tantra, alcohol is used to catalyze the fundamental energy of intoxication; this is the energy that transmutes the duality of the apparent world in advaya—not two. In this way, form, smell, and sound can be perceived literally, as they are, within the realm of mahasukha, or great joy."

Man's natural pursuit is to seek comfort and entertain himself with all kinds of sensual pleasures. He wants a secure home, a happy marriage, stimulating friends, delicious foods, fine clothes, and good wine. But morality generally teaches that this kind of indulgence is not good; we should think of our lives in a broader sense. We should think of our brothers and sisters who lack these things; rather than indulging ourselves, we should share generously with them.

Moralistic thinking tends to see alcohol as belonging to the category of excessive self-indulgences; it might even see drinking as a bourgeois activity. On the other hand, those who like drinking draw a sense of well-being from it and feel it enables them to be warmer and more open with their

Composed during 1972 retreat in Charlemont, Massachusetts.

friends and colleagues. But even they often harbor some sense of guilt about drinking; they fear they might be abusing their bodies and feel deficient in self-respect.

One type of drinker works hard during the day, doing heavy labor in one or another of the physical trades. Such drinkers like to come home and have a drink after work or raise a glass or two in a hearty gathering at the bar. Then there are the more genteel drinkers—business executives and such—who are often in the habit of creating an atmosphere of conviviality in their business relations by breaking out the bottle. The latter type is more likely to have a hidden sense of guilt about alcohol than his proletarian brother celebrating the end of a day's work. Still, in spite of all doubts, inviting somebody for a drink seems to have more life to it than inviting somebody for a cup of tea.

Other people drink to try to kill boredom, much in the same way as they try by smoking. A housewife who has just finished dusting or the wash might sit down and take a drop while contemplating the decor or leafing through the latest fashion and home-improvement magazines. When the baby cries or the doorbell rings, she might take a hefty shot before facing the situation. The bored office worker might keep a flask in his desk so he can take an occasional nip between visits from the boss or his heavy-handed secretary. He might seek relief from the day's ennui through a lunchtime visit to the bar.

People who take drinking seriously relate to it as a refuge from life's hustle and bustle; they also fear they might be becoming alcoholics. In either psychological situation, there is love and hate in their style of drinking, coupled with a sense of going into the unknown. In some cases, this journey into the unknown might already have produced a clarity which, in the present situation, can only be dealt with by drinking. Otherwise the clarity would be too painful.

One of the problems convinced drinkers might be facing is being hounded by the moralistic approach to drinking, which raises the artificial question: should one drink or not? In the grips of this question, one looks to one's friends for reinforcement. Some of them might join one in drinking quite freely. Others will have definite reservations about when and how to drink. The real drinker feels such people are amateurs, since they have never related wholeheartedly with alcohol. Quite often their reservations are just a matter of social form: just as one knows that the place to park one's car is the parking lot, so one has the sense of the proper point beyond which one shouldn't drink. It is all right to drink heavily at parties or testimonial dinners so long as one drinks with one's wife or husband and drives home carefully.

There seems to be something wrong with an approach to alcohol that is based entirely on morality or social propriety. The scruples implied have solely to do with the external effects of one's drinking. The real effect of alcohol is not considered, but only its impact on the social format. On the other hand, a drinker feels that there is something worthwhile in his drinking aside from the pleasure he or she gets out of it. There are the warmth and openness that seem to come from the relaxation of his usual self-conscious style. Also there is the confidence of being able to communicate his perceptions accurately, which cuts through his usual feeling of inadequacy. Scientists find they are able to solve their problems; philosophers have new insights; and artists find clear perception. The drinker experiences greater clarity because he feels more really what he is; therefore daydreams and fantasies can be temporarily put aside.

It seems that alcohol is a weak poison which is capable of being transmuted into medicine. An old Persian folktale tells how the peacock thrives on poison, which nourishes his system and brightens his plumage.

The word *whiskey* comes from the Gaelic *uisgebeatha*, which means "water of life." The Danes have their *aquavit*. The Russian potato produces vodka, the "little water." The traditional names imply that alcohol is at the least harmless, probably medicinal. Harmless or medicinal, the power of alcohol has affected social and psychological structures in most parts of the world throughout history. In Indian mysticism, both Hindu and Buddhist, alcohol is called *amrita*, the potion that is antideath. Birwapa, an Indian *siddha*, won enlightenment when he drank seven gallons of liquor in one afternoon. Mr. Gurdjieff, a spiritual teacher who taught in Europe, spoke of the virtues of "conscious drinking" and insisted that his students do conscious drinking together. Conscious drinking is a real and obvious demonstration of mind over matter. It allows us to relate to the various stages of intoxication: we experience our expectations, the almost devilish delight when the effect begins to be felt, and the final breakdown into frivolity in which habitual boundaries begin to dissolve.

Nevertheless, alcohol can as easily be a death potion as a medicine. The sense of joviality and heartiness can seduce us to relinquish our awareness. But fortunately there is also a subtle depression that goes with drinking. There is a strong tendency to latch onto the heartiness and ignore the depression; this is the ape instinct. It is a great mistake. If we take alcohol merely as a substance that will cheer us up or loosen us up like a sedative, it becomes exceedingly dangerous. It is the same with alcohol as with anything else in life that we relate to only partially.

There is a great difference between alcohol and other inebriants. In contrast with alcohol, such substances as LSD, marijuana, and opium do not bring simultaneous depression. If depression does occur, it is of a purely conceptual nature. But with alcohol, there are always physical symptoms:

weight gain, loss of appetite, increased feeling of solidity (which includes hangovers). There is always the sense that one still has a body. Psychologically, intoxication with alcohol is a process of coming down, rather than, as with the other substances, of going up into space.

Whether alcohol is to be a poison or a medicine depends on one's awareness while drinking. Conscious drinking—remaining aware of one's state of mind—transmutes the effect of alcohol. Here awareness involves a tightening up of one's system as an intelligent defense mechanism. Alcohol becomes destructive when one gives in to the joviality: letting loose permits the poisons to enter one's body. Thus alcohol can be a testing ground. It brings to the surface the latent style of the drinker's neuroses, the style that he is habitually hiding. If his neuroses are strong and habitually deeply hidden, he later forgets what happened when he was drunk or else is extremely embarrassed to remember what he did.

Alcohol's creativity begins when there is a sense of dancing with its effect—when one takes the effects of drink with a sense of humor. For the conscious drinker, or for the *yogi*, the virtue of alcohol is that it brings one down to ordinary reality, so that one does not dissolve into meditation on nonduality. In this case alcohol acts as a longevity potion. Those who are overly involved with the sense that the world is a mirage, an illusion, have to be brought down out of their meditation into a state of nonmeditation to relate with people. In this state, the sights, sounds, and smells of the world become overwhelmingly poignant with their humor. When the yogi drinks, it is his way of accepting the dualistic world of ordinary appearance. The world demands his attention—his relationship and compassion. He is glad and amused to have this invitation to communicate.

For the yogi, alcohol is fuel for relating with his students and with the world in general, as gasoline allows a motorcar to relate with the road. But naturally the ordinary drinker who tries to compete with or imitate this transcendental style of drinking will turn his alcohol into poison. In the *hinayana* teaching of Buddhism, it is recorded that the Buddha reproved a monk who so much as tasted a blade of grass soaked in alcohol. It is necessary to understand that here the Buddha was not condemning the effects of alcohol; he was condemning the attraction toward it, the involvement with it as a temptation.

The conception of alcohol as a temptation of the devil is a highly questionable one. Questioning this conception brings uncertainty as to whether alcohol is allied with good or evil. This uncertainty can create in the drinker a sense of intelligence and fearlessness. It brings him to relate to the present moment as it is. Fearless willingness to be intelligent about what is happening in the face of the unknown is the very energy of transmutation that has been described in the tantric tradition of Buddhism. In the *Guhyasamaja Tantra*, the Buddha says, "That which intoxicates the dualistic mind is the natural antideath potion indeed." In the Buddhist tantra, alcohol is used to catalyze the fundamental energy of intoxication; this is the energy that transmutes the duality of the apparent world into *advaya*—"not two." In this way, form, smell, and sound can be perceived literally, as they are, within the realm of *mahasukha* or great joy. The *Chakrasamvara Tantra* says, "By pure pain without pleasure, one cannot be liberated. Pleasure exists within the calyx of the lotus. This must the yogi nourish." This puts a lot of emphasis on pleasure. But the realization of pleasure comes about through openly relating with pain. Alcohol brings an elation that seems to go beyond all limitations; at the same time it brings the depression of knowing one still has a body and that one's neuroses are heavy upon one. Conscious drinkers might have a glimpse of both of these polarities.

In tantric mysticism, the state of intoxication is called the state of nonduality. This should not be understood as an enticement to entertain oneself, but at the same time, a glimpse of the cosmic orgasm of *mahasukha* is highly possible for the conscious drinker. If one is open enough to surrender the pettiness of attachment to one's personal liberation by accepting the notion of freedom rather than doubting it, one achieves skillful means and wisdom. This is regarded as the highest intoxication.

Practice and Basic Goodness:
A Talk for Children

"As you are growing up it is a good idea to jazz yourselves up—to feel strong and to take pride in yourselves. You don't have to feel inadequate because you are children trying to reach adulthood. Those struggles are not even necessary. You just have to be. In order to do that, you need to develop an attitude of believing in your basic goodness, and you need to practice meditation."

I would like to talk about how we came to be here and why we are Buddhists. It is very simple and straightforward in some sense: you and your parents and I are all following a particular discipline, a particular tradition, called Buddhism. When you go to your school, which is not a Buddhist school, you might find the atmosphere to be somewhat strange. You might want to do things the way others are doing them; and when you come home, you might want to follow your parents' way. On the other hand, you might feel resistance to your parents.

What Buddhism boils down to is that we try to follow the example of the Buddha, who was an Indian—not an Ameri-

Based on a 1978 seminar for children held in Boulder, Colorado.

can Indian, but an Indian Indian. The Buddha was a prince who decided to abandon his palace and his kingdom in order to find out what life is all about. He was looking for the meaning of life, the purpose of life. He wanted to know who and what he was. So he went and practiced meditation, and he ate very little. He meditated for six years, twenty-four hours a day. And at the end of those six years he discovered something: he realized that people don't have to struggle so much. We don't have to give in so much to our hassles, our pain, our discomfort. The Buddha discovered that there is something in us known as *basic goodness*. Therefore, we don't have to condemn ourselves for being bad or naughty. The Buddha taught what he had learned to the rest of mankind. What he taught then—twenty-five hundred years ago—is still being taught and practiced. The important point for us to realize is that we are basically good.

Our only problem is that sometimes we don't actually acknowledge that goodness. We don't see it, so we blame somebody else or we blame ourselves. That is a mistake. We don't have to blame others, and we don't have to feel nasty or angry. Fundamental goodness is always with us, always in us. That is why our education is not difficult. If we have fundamental goodness in us, then knowledge is already a part of us. Therefore, going to school and meditation are just ways of acknowledging that basic goodness.

As you are growing up it is a good idea to jazz yourselves up—to feel strong and to take pride in yourselves. You don't have to feel inadequate because you are children trying to reach adulthood. Those struggles are not even necessary. You just have to *be*. In order to do that, you need to develop an attitude of believing in your basic goodness, and you need to practice meditation. Sitting meditation is a living tradition. We know how the Buddha did it, and we know how to do it ourselves. When you sit like the Buddha, you begin to realize something called *enlightenment*. That is just realizing that there is something very straightforward and very sparkling in you. It is not necessarily "feeling good." It is much better than feeling good: you have a sense of tremendous buoyancy, upliftedness. You feel healthy and simple and strong.

If you would like to ask questions, please do so.

STUDENT: This is a foolish question, but if the Buddha sat for six years, twenty-four hours a day, how did he eat?

TRUNGPA RINPOCHE: Well, he ate very little. According to history he had one meal in the morning—something like our breakfast. And he slept very little. Mostly he just sat. When his friends came to see him, they didn't recognize him at first, because he was so thin. On the morning of the day he attained enlightenment, he was visited by a lady who gave him rice and milk, which energized him. Then he returned to his sitting practice, so to speak, but he wasn't thin from then on. In paintings of the Buddha, like the one you see on the shrine, there are halos around his head. The halo represents the idea of glowing health and glowing greatness.

STUDENT: Rinpoche, could you recommend how long children should sit?

TRUNGPA RINPOCHE: A daily sitting practice would be very good. Hopefully you can do that. I started sitting when I was nine; I used to sit for about forty-five minutes. But due to the circumstances, I think probably seven minutes would be fine—every day. That is quite long enough. If you can only do it once a week, you should try to sit for half an hour. Your parents could sit with you, or you could do it alone. And the place where you sit should be elegant and comfortable. Do you sit at home?

S: Sometimes.

TR: How often? Once a week?

S: After school.

TR: Well, maybe that is a good model. So you could come home and relax that way.

STUDENT: I get depressed a lot, and I want to know if I should sit more.

TRUNGPA RINPOCHE: Yes, you should sit more. That is the whole idea. Particularly when you feel depressed or when you are too excited, you should sit more, because then you have something to work with. That is what the Buddha did. Before he went for his six-year retreat, he was very depressed; he was very unhappy with his whole life. Because he was so depressed, he had something to work on.

STUDENT: When I sit, I usually get restless.

TRUNGPA RINPOCHE: Well, people do—always. That's all right, but don't give in to your restlessness. Just try to hold your posture and come back to your breath. You see, what you are doing is imitating the Buddha. You should hold your head and shoulders upright, like he did. In that way you feel good. When you begin to feel restless, you begin to hunch your head and shoulders. You become restless like an animal. When you sit upright, you are different from an animal. That posture will cut through your restlessness.

STUDENT: When you led all those people out of Tibet, did you just guess which way to go?

TRUNGPA RINPOCHE: No, I didn't quite guess.

S: But when you got lost, did you guess which way to go?

TR: Well, you have a sense of direction and you have a feeling that India is that way. When you have lost your way, you stop for five minutes and sit. After that, you have much clearer vision and you know where to go. You only lose your way if you are distracted. So, if your mind is clear, you know where India is. Then there is little problem. There are trails that go in that direction, and you just follow them.

S: When you were leading people through the snow in the mountains, did you feel calm all the way?

TR: Well, we had to be calm. Otherwise we would lose our way. And we would lose our strength. We also felt very energized. I never felt any doubt; we just went on. So calmness was very important, as well as some kind of strength. We zeroed in on the idea that we were going to do it, and we did it.

S: So your confidence helped you to be strong enough to go over the mountains?

TR: Yes.

STUDENT: In pictures of the Buddha, you usually see three jewels. I don't know what they mean.

TRUNGPA RINPOCHE: The three jewels represent the idea of Buddha's students opening themselves up and making offerings to him. They represent offering one's body, speech, and mind to the Buddha. You are giving yourself to him and to his teachings. These jewels will supposedly give you more riches, more wealth. By giving to the Buddha whatever is precious to you, you attain patience and richness.

STUDENT: On your trip, did you ever run out of food?

TRUNGPA RINPOCHE: Well, we did—absolutely. Did you read about it in the book? Have you read *Born in Tibet?* You should read it. It's some story. [Laughter.] We did run out of food. In the last month or so, we didn't have much to eat. We had to cook our own leather bags. When we got to the lower elevations, we found bamboo and litchis and banana trees. But we passed right by the banana trees; we didn't know they were edible. Nobody had ever seen banana trees before.

S: When you were traveling, did you sit?

TR: Yes, we did. We made a point of doing that. That is how we gained our strength, our energy. Otherwise we would have been destroyed. It was a ten-month journey altogether—very long.

STUDENT: Did any people die on your trip?

TRUNGPA RINPOCHE: Three people died. They were too old to walk. Because our schedule was very tight, we had to walk from morning to evening. Their legs began to hurt and they just collapsed.

STUDENT: Were there any children with you?

TRUNGPA RINPOCHE: Lots of them. It was difficult for mothers with babies, but the older children did fine. Actually, they were the best, because they began to get more and more energized. They gained strength.

Once we were crossing the Chinese highway. We had to time it so that the Chinese soldiers wouldn't see us. Below us was the highway with troops on it. We had to wait on the side of the ridge until dark. We planned to cross all together, in one batch. Just as we were about to cross, a truck went by, and the infants started to cry at the top of their lungs. But the Chinese didn't see us. After we had crossed, somebody swept the road with a broom so that the Chinese wouldn't find our footprints.

STUDENT: How tall were the eight biggest men—the ones who used to lie down and make a path for the others through the snow?

TRUNGPA RINPOCHE: Well, they were not particularly big. They were tough, that's all.

S: Are they still alive?

TR: Yes—although we started with three hundred people,

and a lot of them were captured. Only twenty-nine of us escaped.

STUDENT: Are the Chinese and the Tibetan Buddhists still at war, or is the war over? Are they still shooting at each other?

TRUNGPA RINPOCHE: No, not at this point. The Chinese destroyed or exiled most of the Buddhist leaders, so now they have no one left to fight.

STUDENT: Since you were meditating on the trip, you don't feel very rebellious or angry at the Chinese, do you?

TRUNGPA RINPOCHE: Well, not particularly. What happened with the Chinese was like a rainstorm: you can't get angry at it. It was a timely situation. If the Chinese weren't in Tibet, I wouldn't be here.

STUDENT: Why do people look up to Christ? What is it in him that they like?

TRUNGPA RINPOCHE: Well, he was very heroic. And he was inspired, as we know. He sacrificed his life for the sake of other people. Crowds gathered to hear him talk on Sunday morning. He was a gentle person, a good person. There were a lot of other good people apart from Christ. There was Mohammed, for example. Who else?

S: King David.

TR: Yes, and lots of other people who have done similar things.

STUDENT: On your trip, did the Chinese ever try to track you down?

TRUNGPA RINPOCHE: Yes, they certainly did. I think they followed us all the way, but we outsmarted them. They are still supposed to be looking for me, actually. I have a friend who went to the Chinese embassy in London. He saw my photograph there with a price on my head.

STUDENT: What caused the war between the Chinese and the Buddhists?

TRUNGPA RINPOCHE: Well, the communists don't like meditation practice. They think it is a waste of time. They think that people should be working all the time. Meditation produces too much personal strength. The communists want to develop group strength, not personal strength. They do not believe in the basic goodness of the individual; they believe in the basic goodness of the group. That is why it is called communism; that's it in a nutshell.

Well, maybe we should close at this point. Thank you, children, for being so patient and for not being restless. Your patience is quite remarkable. It must be due to your practice of meditation. Please keep sitting, okay? And study Buddhism more, and try to make friends with your parents—if you can. [Laughter.] Regard them as friends rather than as relatives. That is a very important point. Thank you.

Dharma Poetics

"When we talk about poets and poetics altogether, we are talking in terms of expressing ourselves so thoroughly, so precisely, that we don't just mumble our words, mumble our minds, mumble our bodies. Being in the poetic world, we have something to wake up and excite ourselves. There is a sense of gallantry and there is a tremendous, definite attitude of no longer being afraid of threats of any kind. We begin to help ourselves to appreciate our world, which is already beautiful."

In discussing poetics, we are not bound to the theme of written poetry. Poetics also includes one's vision, hearing, and feeling, altogether. So, we are not talking about writing poetry alone; we are talking about a complete, comprehensive realization of the phenomenal world—seeing things as they are. We are talking in terms of the poetic way of eating one's food and drinking one's tea. We could call this approach *dharma poetics. Dharma,* as you know, is the teachings of the Buddha. Basically, the word *dharma* means "norm," or some form of experiencing reality properly.

We could speak of three stages of poetics. The first is the rejection stage. We reject habitual patterns which are caused

Based on discussion with Naropa Institute poetics students, 1982.

by ego-oriented situations, such as the desire to develop aggression, passion, and ignorance. We have to free ourselves from these patterns. For instance, if we do not wash a piece of cloth completely clean, we will be unable to dye it another color, such as bright red, bright green, or bright blue. The point is that we have to have a sense of purity and giving up before we can put the cloth that we have woven into the various dyes that we would like to use. We first have to wash it thoroughly.

It is similar with our minds and our bodies. We have to go through some sense of purification, natural purification. This process might include letting go of our personal trips, letting go of desires, and letting go of any philosophy that has been taught to us.

In the second stage, we can aspire to the basic meaning of poetics. There are two main kinds of poetics: rejuvenating poetics and growing-old poetics. Between the two, many other kinds of poetics could arise. We could appreciate the sun, the moon, the green grass, the flowers, the brooks, and the mountains. We could appreciate rainstorms; we could appreciate snowfalls; we could appreciate our father and mother. We could appreciate the whole world. Or, for that matter, we could mock them. Mocking is also acceptable— always acceptable. We could mock April's snowfall; we could mock our father or mother treating us badly.

In general, poetics is based on the idea that first we see our universe very clearly, very precisely, and very thoroughly. We are not fooled by anybody. That seems to be the basic notion of poetics here.

I could give you one poem as an example; it is not memorized, but composed on the spot:

> Father's love is good.
> Did I borrow from my mother?

Nonetheless, I still remain
chrysanthemum.

STUDENT: You said there are two kinds of poetics: rejuvenating and growing-old. What did you mean by that?

TRUNGPA RINPOCHE: Well, either you have seen enough of the world already, or you're about to see the world as it is growing up. It's like the difference between a good spring and a good autumn.

S: Or a young poet and an old poet?

TR: That's right. Very much so.

S: What is it that the old poet knows that the young poet doesn't?

TR: Well, what you just said is in itself poetry. Ask yourself! You see, the trick is that I'm not going to help you particularly. You have to discover it for yourself.

S: That's helpful. [Laughter.]

TR: Being less helpful is more helpful than being helpful.

STUDENT: I feel that there is some beauty in imperfection. If you did wash your cloth completely, and you dyed it a pure color, then your color would be pure, but it would only be one color.

TRUNGPA RINPOCHE: It wouldn't necessarily be only one color. You could dye your cloth lots of colors. And each time you did, a different kind of smile and a different delight would take place. We are not talking about completely totalitarian poetics; we are talking about poetics that can encompass multilateral situations—different types for different people. But at the beginning we have to clean up first. That is always the case. Having cleaned up, then lots of colors can come through. It is like a well-cleaned mirror: many things can be reflected in it.

Now, without delaying too much, I would like to continue to discuss the evolution from purification and a sense of longing for liberation, which we talked about earlier on, and add a third stage.

The three stages that we are discussing are actually connected with a basic sense of joy. Sometimes joy means having one's individual way of not working genuinely with oneself and instead working toward a sense of indulgency. But here joy means *not* indulging oneself. That is the first stage, which we described earlier as purifying oneself and rejecting one's habitual patterns.

In other words, joy means that our perception of the world can be clarified. The best poetic philosophy, in this case, is to have a sense of precision and accuracy in how we see the universe, how we actually perceive the universe, which is the second stage.

When we clarify our perception, we are not fooled by green, yellow, red, blue, pink, or orange. We are not fooled by them, and we are also not fooled by mountains, brooks, flowers, or bees. I leave it up to your imagination to come up with all sorts of things like that. We are not fooled by our father, our mother, our sisters, our brothers, or our lovers, either. All these things could create central themes for poetry, but at the same time, these things could create obstacles; they could create a blindfoldedness.

Perhaps there is more to say about joy here. Joy is something that we see, something that we experience properly, fully, and thoroughly in the universe, in our world. In other words, we do not pull long faces; we begin to appreciate this world that we're living in. This world is a lovely world, a wonderful world. The Judeo-Christian tradition would say it's a gift of God. In the Buddhist tradition it is said to be a result of our karmic magnificence. In any case, joy is always there.

The third stage is that we must be clear and pure in our speech and our minds. When we talk about poets and poetics altogether, we are talking in terms of expressing ourselves so thoroughly, so precisely, that we don't just mumble our words, mumble our minds, mumble our bodies. Being in the poetic world, we have something to wake up and excite in ourselves. There is a sense of gallantry and there is a tremendous, definite attitude of no longer being afraid of threats of any kind. We begin to help ourselves to appreciate our world, which is already beautiful. So, I think that's the point.

STUDENT: You talked about many things in our everyday experience that we shouldn't be fooled by. What did you mean by that?

TRUNGPA RINPOCHE: Well, I think it's a question of simply just being on the dot. We shouldn't let ourselves be used by somebody else as part of their trip—their egomania or philosophy. We should simply remain as what we are. Just on the dot. Philosophy in this case could be anything— religious, sociological, or political. The idea is that we should not let ourselves be subject to any experience, unless we experience it properly, thoroughly, by knowing what we're doing.

S: By knowing that we are laying our philosophy on the mountain or the brooks?

TR: Well, you can praise the mountain, you can praise the sky; you can do those things. But any trips you lay on things, you have to let go of.

S: And then there's joy?

TR: Yes. If you are unhappy—not joyful—then you buy a lot of trips. You still have a long face, but you always buy it when somebody presents some stuff to you. In this case we

are saying that once you're joyful and you feel gallantry—
you feel who you are and you feel good—then you will automatically know who's trying to fool you and who's trying to
help you.

S: How much energy should you expend trying to figure
out if someone's fooling you or if you're fooling yourself?

TR: Well, that's very complicated, you know, because
sometimes you think you are the other and the other also
thinks they are you. So I think the best approach there is to
enjoy mountains, rivers, forests, snow, rain, and hailstorms
by yourself. You will find some poetic way of saving yourself
that way. Actually, I think that's what mountains are for,
originally. Brooks are there for you to do that—and trees
and jungles as well. So be yourself by yourself. I'm sure you
will compose magnificent poetry if you do that.

ALLEN GINSBERG: I sometimes find it difficult to con-
ceive of enjoying myself when I'm ill or in pain. I wonder
what it would be like to be very old and on the road in Jor-
dan with shrapnel and cluster bombs flying around, feeling
the end of family, the end of home. I wonder what possibility there would be of writing appreciative poetry under extremely painful situations and conditions, such as old age,
sickness, and death.

TRUNGPA RINPOCHE: Well, pain goes with pleasure, always. That's a classic remark. When you feel pain, it is because you feel joyful at the same time. Why do you wear
sunglasses, which are black? You wear them because there is
lots of light coming toward you. Do you understand the
logic? The notion of frustration also goes along with that.
You feel a sense of both alternatives, always. When you are
in the worst pain, you sometimes feel the best happiness.
Have you ever experienced that? We read about that in the
stories of Milarepa and Marpa—all the Kagyü lineage poets.

AG: Well, is it the steadiness of mind cultivated by meditation practice that keeps you from total disillusion, depression, and physical pain?

TR: I think there has to be some kind of spark, some kind of explosion of joy, happening in the midst of pain. It usually happens *more* in the midst of pain.

AG: Do you think that's actually happening to people who are under really horrible circumstances, for example in Lebanon?

TR: Yes, I think so. Because there is so much chaos, therefore there is so much tranquility. Tranquility is relative to chaos. It's Einstein's philosophy.

STUDENT: Do you feel there's something lacking in American poetry because we don't have a meditative tradition?

TRUNGPA RINPOCHE: Well, I think American poets are getting there, basically speaking. But I must say American poets do need some kind of meditative discipline in order to appreciate the phenomenal world, in order to appreciate that the greenness of green is beautiful, the blueness of the sky is lovely, and the whiteness of the clouds is so fantastic. Maybe poets spend too much time writing poetry. They have to see the vividness of the world.

America is a wonderful place. You have the highest mountains, beautiful lakes, and extraordinary greenery and fruit. You have everything in this country. You should be proud of your country, then you'll see the beauty of America—if you become a poet.

STUDENT: Rinpoche, I've heard the saying that "suffering is the broom that sweeps away the cause of suffering." When you speak about sparks of pleasure in pain, is that the quality you're referring to?

TRUNGPA RINPOCHE: Well said. You must be studying Buddhism! [Laughter.] You must be studying vajrayana.

S: It was Situ Rinpoche who said that.

TR: Oh yes, that's good. Thank you very much.

13

Green Energy

"When we relate to money properly, it is no longer a mere token of exchange or of abstract energy; it is also a discipline. No longer hooked by it as a medicine that has become a drug, we can deal with it in a practical, earthy way as a master deals with his tools."

In dealing with money, we are constantly involved in a kind of chaos. This results from a break in the relationship between the earth and oneself. Relating to the earth means knowing when to act practically and directly; it means actually feeling a kinship with whatever work is being done. We rarely have this feeling when it comes to money matters.

Money is basically a very simple thing. But our attitude toward it is overloaded, full of preconceived ideas that stem from the development of a self-aggrandizing ego and its manipulative processes. The mere act of handling money—just pieces of paper—is viewed as a very serious game. It is almost like building a sand castle and then selling tickets for admission to it. The difference between playing as a child and playing as an adult is that in the adult's case, money is

Originally composed in 1976 for *Harper's* special edition on money.

involved. Children don't think about money, whereas adults would like to charge admission to their solemn construction.

Even when we try to regard money as insignificant—as merely a credential or a token of our creative capacity or our practicality—because money is connected with the energy arising from our preconceptions, it takes on great significance. We may even feel embarrassment about money—it is somewhat too close to the heart. We try to call it something else—"bread" or "bucks"—to relieve that feeling. Or, we choose to think of money as our lifeline, as a source of security: its abstract quality represents some unspeakable aspect of our personality. We may say, for example: "I have gone bankrupt and lost heart"; "I'm a solid citizen with a steady bank account"; "I have so much money that there is no room for simplicity in my life."

The energy money takes on makes a tremendous difference in the process of communication and relationship. If a friend suddenly refuses to pay his check at a restaurant, a feeling of resentment or separation automatically arises in relation to him. If one buys a friend a cup of tea—which is just a cup, hot water, and tea—somehow a factor of meaningfulness gets added.

It seems to me that it is worthwhile to work with the negative aspects of money in order to gain some understanding about ourselves. We must try to discover how to view this embarrassing and potent commodity as a part of ourselves that we cannot ignore. When we relate to money properly, it is no longer a mere token of exchange or of our abstract energy; it is also a discipline. No longer hooked by it as a medicine that has become a drug, we can deal with it in a practical, earthy way, as a master deals with his tools.

14

Manifesting Enlightenment

"*If you wait too long, in the Christian tradition, as well as in the Buddhist tradition, nothing happens. For example, the concept of 'Holy Ghost' and the concept of 'first thought, best thought' simply pounce on you, rather than you having to wait for them. This requires a certain sense of bravery: you have to be willing to jump in right away. Whenever there is any inspiration, you just jump in. That is why it is said that 'first thought is best thought.' Just jump in!*"

Enlightenment is a rather tall subject, and I would like to keep my discussion of it rather simple. The word for enlightenment in Sanskrit is *bodhi,* which means "awake." When the word *bodhi* is made into a noun it becomes *buddha.* Buddha refers to someone who has developed an awake state of being. When we talk about awake here, it has nothing to do with being physically awake as opposed to sleeping. Rather, awake means being basically realized, being able to see the pain of the world and being able to see the way out of the world of suffering.

After the Buddha's attainment of enlightenment, he spent

Talk given at Naropa Institute's third Conference on Buddhist and Christian Meditation, 1983.

seven weeks contemplating how he could communicate such an experience of wakefulness to others. I suppose we could correlate that with Christ spending such an extensive time in the desert—some people even say Christ went to Tibet, or at least to Kashmir.

The Buddha discovered and taught that human beings are in fact capable of being woken up. The state of being awake has two main qualities: the first, *karuna* in Sanskrit, is softness, gentleness, which we call "compassion"; the other, *upaya* in Sanskrit, is called "skillful means." The compassion aspect is connected with oneself, and the skillful means aspect is connected with how to deal with others. Compassion and skillful means put together is what is known as *egolessness*. Nonego means being free from any kind of bondage, free from any fixed motivation to hold onto one's basic being.

We have a tendency to hold onto concepts and perceptions of all kinds. We must admit that tendency and realize that such situations bind us to the *lower realms:* the hell realm, the hungry ghost realm, and the animal realm. I suppose in the Christian tradition these realms are connected with the idea of sin. In the Buddhist tradition we don't talk about punishment as such, and the concept of original sin does not exist. Instead, Buddhism speaks about *habitual patterns.* For example, when a dog sees a person, it wants to bite, it wants to bark; when a flea jumps on your body, it wants to bite; when a human being sees another human being, he wants to kiss, and so forth. That kind of instinctual response is the definition of habitual patterns. When a person gets stuck in habitual patterns, then he exists in the lower realms of his passion, aggression, and delusion.

There are all kinds of habitual tendencies that are connected with holding onto what we are. People get divorced because they think they might find a better mate. People change restaurants because they think they might get cheaper and better food. The habitual patterns of ego work that way. The notion of enlightenment is a sense of freedom from those patterns. And the way to attain that freedom is by means of the sitting practice of meditation.

In sitting practice, we look at our minds, and we maintain good posture. When we combine body and mind that way, we find ourselves emulating the Buddha—the way to *be* properly. Then we begin to develop sympathy toward ourselves rather than just holding on. We begin to develop a sense of softness. We can see this in the way that Buddhists talk softly and walk mindfully.

Beyond sitting meditation itself, we begin to expand our experience of softness and mindfulness to other activities, such as shopping, cooking, cleaning, and any activities that we do. We begin to find that things are workable rather than hassles or problems. We find that life is worth living. And we begin to treat ourselves better; we wear good clothes, eat good food, and constantly smile. We cheer up, and we realize there is something good about life. And we also realize that others can be brought into our society, our world.

We can conduct ourselves mindfully and appreciate the phenomenal world. We can realize that the hassles in our lives are not created by others; rather, we create these hassles for ourselves. Therefore, we can remove them and appreciate our world. I would suggest to everybody: let us be aware of our being, let us celebrate as we experience our lives, and smile at least three times a day. Thank you.

I apologize if this sounds like a sermon. If you would like to ask questions, you are more than welcome.

QUESTION: I am so delighted to be here as a Christian, with your hospitality making it all possible. My heart is full of love of the spirit that makes this possible. We have so much to learn from each other. I have so much to learn. I am told that this meeting at Naropa has been made possible by you because of a meeting that you had with Thomas Merton. If you care to share them, I would be delighted to hear your impressions of that meeting, since we bear the fruits here today.

TRUNGPA RINPOCHE: Thank you. Father Merton's visit to Southeast Asia took place when I was in Calcutta. He was invited by a group that had a philosophy of spiritual shopping, and he was the only person who felt that it was full of confusion. He felt there was a sense of ignorance there, but nonetheless he joined them. We had dinner together, and we talked about spiritual materialism a lot. We drank many gin and tonics. I had the feeling that I was meeting an old friend, a genuine friend.

In fact, we planned to work on a book containing selections from the sacred writings of Christianity and Buddhism. We planned to meet either in Great Britain or in North America. He was the first genuine person I met from the West.

After meeting Father Merton, I visited several monasteries and nunneries in Great Britain, and at some of them I was asked to give talks on meditation, which I did. I was very impressed.

When I was studying at Oxford, I had a tutor who was a Belgian priest, a Jesuit priest, who had studied in Sri Lanka. He knew Sanskrit and he read a lot of the Buddhist *sutras* and the commentaries that go with them. I was very impressed and moved by the contemplative aspect of Christianity and by the monasteries themselves. Their life-styles and the way they conducted themselves convinced me that the only way to join the Christian tradition and the Buddhist tradition together would be by bringing together Christian contemplative practice with Buddhist meditative practice.

QUESTION: Sir, Tenshin Anderson Sensei spoke the other day about a still place in the center where the buddhas live—where one experiences the pain of all sentient beings, the suffering of all sentient beings. And he said that from there arise outcroppings, or clouds that begin to form and rise. He said that this is the essence of compassion and skillful means, and that from this arising you can go out into the world and do good for all sentient beings. This made me think about "first thought, best thought." Could you say something about "first thought, best thought," and compassionate action in the world.

TRUNGPA RINPOCHE: I think it is a question of not waiting. If you wait too long, in the Christian tradition, as well as in the Buddhist tradition, nothing happens. For example, the concept of "Holy Ghost" and the concept of "first thought, best thought" simply pounce on you, rather than you having to wait for them. This requires a certain sense of bravery: you have to be willing to jump in right away. Whenever there is any inspiration, you just jump in. That is why it is said that "first thought is best thought." Just jump in!

QUESTION: In relation to that, we have talked about being compulsive in wanting to help, about jumping out too soon and wanting to change someone. If someone is suffering, you want to *stop* that suffering, but that might be compulsive and could just cause more harm. Could you say more about the distinction between true compassionate action and compulsive behavior?

TRUNGPA RINPOCHE: It is a question of sneezing and wiping your nose. You sneeze spontaneously, and after that you wipe your nose.

Q: Thank you very much!

QUESTION: First I would like to say that I thought that was a very nice Christian talk you gave.

TRUNGPA RINPOCHE: Thank you.

Q: But being here and meeting many Christians, I find that they are always very defensive about the idea that Buddhists do not believe in any kind of reality or concept of God. And I try to pacify them by saying that I find in my readings that the Buddhists simply use different words. They capitalize the word *Self*, or they capitalize the word *That*, or they capitalize the word *Suchness*. I assume that has some special significance.

But today I had an interesting experience. I met a person from the Orthodox tradition who became a Buddhist, and that person communicated to me something you once said in his presence, which was that you had a certain affinity with the Orthodox understanding of the reality that the idea of God represents. I would like to hear you say something about that, and how you understand that whole idea.

TR: The Orthodox tradition was actually the saving grace in my life at Oxford because its followers understand the notion of meditation, and they understand that meditation is not just doing *nothing* but also involves radiating one's openness. The contemplative traditions within both Judaism and Christianity, particularly the Jewish Chasidic tradition and also the Orthodox Christian Prayer of the Heart, which I've studied a little bit, seem to be the ground for Eastern and Western philosophy to join together. It is not so much a question of dogma, but it is a question of *heart;* that is where the common ground lies. One of these days I am going to take my students to Mount Athos to see how the Orthodox monks conduct themselves.

QUESTION: I'd be interested in any comments you might have about the practice of deity yoga and how the visualization of deities brings about a change in consciousness.

TRUNGPA RINPOCHE: What kind of consciousness are you talking about?

Q: The change that's produced by the deity yoga, by the practice of the deity yoga, from our normal awareness of the world. The question I'm asking is, where does this lead; what type of consciousness does this produce?

TR: Everybody is a deity here. It is very simple. I think one of the basic points is to realize the ultimate concept of sacredness. *Sacred* in Sanskrit is *adhishthana,* which also means "blessing." Adhishthana gives you open heart and a sense of wakefulness at once. It is taking place right now while we are having a conversation. Got it?

Q: Thank you, sir.

TR: Well, unfortunately, ladies and gentlemen, there is something called time, and we are running out of it, so we might stop here. I would like to thank everybody who took part in this, and especially the organizers of this conference. All of you have been so kind and genuine and good. Hopefully you can return again and contribute more, if you can. That will be a portion of the cake of saving the world. Thank you very much.

Appendixes

The Pön Way of Life

The study of Pön, the native, pre-Buddhist religion of Tibet, is a vast and largely untreated subject. Unfortunately, accurate information concerning higher spiritual training in Pön is extremely difficult to obtain; materials that are presently available contain only sketchy data, obscured by overlays of popular Buddhism. Moreover, in making inquiries of present-day Pön priests, one finds that they speak a great deal in Buddhist terms, drawing parallels between the highlights of their doctrine and Buddhist teachings.

An investigation of the Pön religion is further complicated by the existence in Tibet of "white Pön," which amounts to a "Pönized" Buddhism. "White Pön" is basically an adopted form of Buddhism, but the Buddha is called Shenrap (see below); the Buddhist *vajra* is replaced by a counterclockwise *svastika*;* and the bodhisattva is called *yungdrung sempa,* that is, *svastikasattva.* Where a text mentions *dharma,* the word *Pön* is substituted. There are Pön equivalent names for all the buddhas and bodhisattvas, and also

---

*The svastika (or *swastika* as it is often pronounced) in Pön represents an unchanging and indestructible quality. In this, it is like the Buddhist vajra, but it differs in that it also connotes richness and plenty. It is often used as a symbol of wealth, appearing as a decoration on an individual's *Chuglha bag*—a bag containing objects sacred to the god of wealth.

for the ten stages—or *bhumis* in Sanskrit—of the bodhisattva path. Many contemporary Pön believers are therefore not good sources of information concerning the pure tradition of their religion. In fact, most of the original Pön texts were eventually destroyed or fell subject to heavy Buddhist editing. In the absence of surviving Pön philosophical sources, the cosmological understanding of Pön must be reconstructed from ritual texts that were left intact owing to their assimilation by Buddhism. Nevertheless, some Pön texts have survived, and it is possible to derive the fundamentals of Pön belief from these.

Pön, which in Tibetan means "way of life," is traditionally interpreted in the sense of "basic law." The Tibetan name for Tibet is Pö, which is basically the same word. Moreover, until about the seventh century, Tibet was referred to by its inhabitants as Pön, Pö being adopted only later. This is verified by ancient scrolls found in caves in Afghanistan early in this century, as well as by ancient Khotanese scrolls which tell of taxes paid to "the great king of Pön." Thus the name of the Tibetan religion was, at least archaically, synonymous with the nation itself.

The higher teachings of Pön were transmitted to the Tibetans by the sage Shenrap Miwo. *Shen* means "heavenly"; *rap* means "supreme one"; and *miwo* means "great man." Shenrap lived long before the Buddha. The Shenrap myth refers to the Buddha, the teacher of wisdom; to Gesar, the teacher of war; to the Lord of Taksik, the teacher of the law of wealth; and so forth. All these are considered incarnations of Shenrap. The work of Shenrap still exists in Tibet in the form of some four hundred volumes, but it has undergone heavy Buddhist editing. A few of the books that have not fallen into Buddhist hands give some clue as to how the practitioner should proceed on the path of Pön.

Pön religion is concerned with the creation of the universe in such a way as to consecrate the existence of the country, customs, and habits of the Tibetan people. This is in contrast to the spirituality of Buddhism, which arises in the far more abstract context of psychological evolution.

The spirituality of Pön is founded in a cosmological reality: nine gods created the world, a world in which birth, death, marriage, and sickness all have their place. If the worshiper can attune himself to those gods through various ritualistic ceremonies, and through an understanding of these ceremonies, then he is in a position to fulfill whatever is demanded of him by the cosmic order. The acquisition of spiritual understanding in Pön is based on the concept of *tendrel*, which means "cosmic law." This is similar to the Buddhist term *nidana*. Both concepts present the flow of events as a causal enchainment. But whereas the Buddhist concept suggests the matter-of-fact nature of fate, tendrel gives much more the idea of an influenceable agency. According to Pön, anyone who attunes himself, through the appropriate rites and practices, to the movement of the interdependence of events is not in danger of being rejected by it. Understanding this interdependence, he can read its signs. By invoking the name of the supreme Pön deity in the appropriate manner, and also by including repetitions of his own name, he can call the gods to himself as allies and defenders.

The supreme divine principle of Pön is referred to as Yeshen. This supreme deity has the same quality of cosmic totality that is found in most theistic religions. *Ye* means "primordial" or "original"; *shen* means "divine," "heavenly," or "spiritual" but also has an anthropomorphic implication. The impression is of a divine ancestor. *Shen* also has the sense of "friend" or "ally," so a benign quality is added. The ancestor aspect also brings the feeling of the richness of age along with the sense of divinity. Yeshen is seen as passive and peaceful, accommodating the idea of a final peaceful rest for the worshiper.

The energetic aspect of the sphere of the divine is represented by another principle—Se. Se, who is primarily vengeful in character, communicates directly with man. He creates the link between the absolute, divine plane and the relative plane of man. The point is that the practitioner of Pön must acquire the ability to see the Yeshen quality in every life situation. If he is able to do this, guidance for the further application of his practice comes from Se, who points him in the appropriate spiritual direction.

Se is a powerful warrior; the Pön worshiper calls him god (*lha*). The national king of Tibet also used *lha* for his title, partaking as well in the image of powerful warrior. In ancient times, the capital of Tibet was thus named Lhasa (*sa* means "place"), identifying the seat of the king with the seat of the god.

At this point it would perhaps be most useful to give some impression of the methods used for relating with Se and achieving union with Yeshen. Pön, unlike the religious outgrowths of the Aryan culture—especially Hinduism, Buddhism, and Jainism in their quasi-popular forms—gives little heed to the pursuit of salvation through the practice of austerities. Pön philosophy speaks of Yeshen as being reflected in the interplay between heaven and earth. Thus the Pön aspirant seeks magical power through union with the Yeshen nature as manifested in mountains, trees, lakes, and rivers—all of which are impressively present in Tibet. There is a strong orientation toward waterfalls, falling snow, clouds, and mist arising from the deep valleys, since all these are regarded as activities of Yeshen. Belief in the magic of these natural features is paramount.

In attempting to commune with Yeshen, the practitioner must first find the highest peak in the locale. He invokes the name of Yeshen in the *lhasang* practice, which is a purifying ceremony often performed on auspicious occasions (even by Buddhists) in Tibet.

To prepare for a lhasang, a fire is made of cedar needles. Offerings are made of the "three whites" (curd, milk, and butter); the "three sweets" (brown sugar, crystal sugar, and honey); as well as offerings of *tsampa* rubbed in butter with popped barley and chalices of barley beer, tea, and milk. Yeshen, Se, and the eight *dégyés* (messengers of Se) are thought to descend from heaven on the smoke of the fire. The cedar is Se's tree, and its wood and smoke are considered ritually pure. The ceremony is intended to bring the divine down into the sphere of human life, as well as to elevate the particular occasion into the sphere of the divine. The burning of the cedar needles is one of the main means of communicating with Yeshen. The devotee becomes absorbed in the smoke of the ritual fire. Certain messages are read from the patterns of the rising smoke; for example, slowly, gently rising white smoke signifies acceptance, while dark smoke that is constantly interrupted by wind signifies obstacles.

There are nine cosmos-creating deities (including Se himself), which figure as part of the Se principle. Only through the mediation of Se, or the other figures who manifest his principle, can the worshiper communicate with Yeshen. There is the sense that, if properly appealed to, Se could approach Yeshen to redispose the ultimate energy of the universe in a way more favorable to the worshiper. The other eight deities are the messengers, or dégyés, of Se. The dégyés might more accurately be regarded as types, or principles, than as individual beings, since each may have many local manifestations. Each dégyé also has a retinue of minions, attendants, helpers, and so on who act on its intentions.

The nature of these Pön divinities can be gathered from their associated practices and iconography. A general iconographical feature of Se and the dégyés is the *per,* a kimono-like garment reaching to the ankles with wide, triangular sleeves and a pleat over each hip. The per was the garment of ancient Tibetan royalty. The warlike dégyés wear armor beneath the per and helmets pennanted in their particular color. The pennants vary according to the status of the figure. Se wears a white per with crystal armor and helmet. White is associated with divinity; it is pure and contains all the other colors. He rides a white horse with turquoise wings.

The only female dégyé is Lu, who is associated with water. Bringing rain, she also brings fertility. Thus she is the patron deity of women, especially young maidens. Lakes and sources of springs where shrines have been built are sacred to her. Lu punishes with leprosy, rheumatism, and skin diseases. She can be propitiated with offerings of the three whites and three sweets. Lu is associated with snakes, blue-gray horses, and blue-gray mules. She wears a gown of feathers and seamless watersilk representing mist. She rides a blue horse with white stripes in water designs, and she holds a crystal vase filled with gems.

Tsen is the god of fire. He has the power of instant destruction. He is associated with speed and the accomplishment of actions—especially destructive actions. He does not kill his enemies externally, but, because of the swiftness of his horse and his quickness to anger, he is able to instantly enter his enemy's body through the mouth or anus. Tsen is the patron deity of bandits and warriors. Harms associated with him are heart attack and death by accident. He is offended by making fire in inappropriate places, by roasting meat, or in general, by creating disturbances or disharmony in any particular environment. Offerings to Tsen are goat's blood and goat's meat. He is associated with brown horses and jackals. Tsen wears copper armor beneath his red per and rides a red roan. The general feeling of the image is of blood and fire. His moment par excellence for striking is at sunset. He holds a scimitar and a lasso.

Another dégyé is Therang, who is thought to be embodied in boulders and ashes as well as in dice. He brings success in games, particularly dice, but also any board games. In ancient warfare, he was thought to guide the trajectories of catapulted boulders. Fever and dizziness are associated with Therang. The appropriate offering to him is popped barley with milk. He is the patron god of children and blacksmiths and is also somewhat associated with rain. Therang rides a goat and wears a goatskin over his black per. He carries a bellows and a hammer.

Dü is associated with darkness. He brings bad luck unless propitiated with offerings of leftovers. He is connected with crows and black pigs. Dü rides a black horse with a white blaze. He wears iron armor and helmet and a black per. He holds a sword and a spear with a black banner. Fastened to his saddle are a waterbag filled with poison; a long black board with a handle inscribed with his victim's names; and a ball of multicolored thread which has a life of its own and can leap from its place and bind up a victim in an excruciating matter.

Chuglha is the god of wealth. He rewards thrift with prosperity and punishes waste with poverty. He can also bring rheumatism, ulcer, and swelling diseases. He is the patron deity of merchants and of the household and is offered butter and grain. He is associated with the earth, as well as with sheep, yaks, and horses. Chuglha rides a yellow horse or a lion. He wears a golden per over golden armor, and a golden hat with four sides in the stylized form of flower petals. He carries a multicolored, cylinder-shaped victory banner in his right hand and a scroll in the left. He vomits gems.

Nyen is the god of the Tibetan folk culture and the patron of rulers and all patriots. He is associated with the mountains. He is offered cheese, the three whites, the three sweets, and spikelets of grain plants. He is infringed against by chopping down any trees that may be held sacred locally and by digging up sacred ground; he is also offended by the smell of burnt food and by the beams of torches or lamps cast on the tops of hills or mountains consecrated to him. He punishes by magnifying physical weaknesses and causing domestic chaos. The horse and deer (especially the musk deer) are his sacred animals, as well as quadrupeds in general and also birds. His female counterpart is associated with storms and weather. The color of Nyen's armor and per vary locally, but are most often white. He carries a white pennant banner. He also carries either a platter or vase of jewels. The color of his horse also varies with locale.

Za is the god of psychological energy, lightning, hailstorms, and, more recently, electricity. Disturbed, he can addle the senses or cause epileptic fits and madness. He can be offended by interrupting anything continuous—for example, by cutting rope or by ruining paint or ink. He is mollified by offerings of goat's meat and goat's blood. He is the patron of magicians and is associated with dragons. Za rides an angry crocodile. Each of his eighteen faces—he has one for each kind of mythical lightning dragon—is topped by a raven's head that shoots out lightning bolts. He is six-armed and holds a victory banner, a snake lasso, a bag of poisonous water, a bow, and a bundle of arrows. Za has a large mouth in his belly, and his body is covered with eyes.

Drala is the god of war and patron of warlords and warriors. He is somewhat identified with storms and storm clouds. He is offended by the mistreatment of weapons. Drala punishes by humiliation and scandal, insomnia and nightmare, and even by loss of one's *la*, or "soul." He is offered barley beer, tea, and the three whites and three sweets. The white yak, horse, eagle, and raven are sacred to him. Drala rides a horse, usually reddish brown. He wears armor and helmet of lacquered metal and a red per. Eighteen pennants fly from his helmet. He holds a long-hoisted flag with eighteen ribbons flying at its edge and wears a belt which holds a bow and arrows, a lasso, an axe, a spear, a dagger, a sword, and other instruments of war. Drala emanates a tiger from his body, a black bear with a white heart from one of his legs, a jackal from each eye, and a hawk and eagle from his head.

Having given an impression of the divinities and their powers, according to Pön belief, an account of some of the customs and practices relating to the life situations of the Pön believer will give further insight into the world of Pön. According to Pön tradition, when a house is to be built, the site should be chosen by a person known for his wisdom and understanding. There are four main elements to be looked for. The building must be situated so that a mountain of Nyen is in the back, that is, to the west. This mountain is called the *lhari*, the "mountain of god." This should be a rocky mountain, preferably covered with red lichen, the whole resembling a great red bird. The house is thus protected, like a child in its mother's lap.

There should also be a mountain on the front side, but not so high as the one in back. It should be somewhat chalky in composition, ideally resembling a white tiger. On the right there should be a river running in an open valley, which, by the shape of its course, should resemble a dragon. On the left should be a screen of mountains resembling a tortoise's back. The tops and ridges of this northern range should not be jagged but should present a solid mass, since spaces sharply gapping its silhouette are said to represent the teeth of death. This could bring death to the family. Any decayed or dead trees around the site portend accident and are cut down, if not found to be the haunt of some local god.

The traditional first step in approaching the site is to build a tower, or *sekhar*, on top of the lhari. The tower is intended as a shrine to Se, the local Nyen, or any other dégyé that is thought to be powerful in the area. The tower invites their blessing on the site. In the ceremony for consecrating the tower, a wool cord is extended in the four directions. This acts as a conductor for Se when he descends from heaven. Certain areas around the tower are designated as sacrosanct; no one goes there unless to make an offering. The follower of Pön considers birth to be extremely sacred. Nevertheless, women were considered impure, since they represent the temptation of passion. Thus, a mother-to-be is required to lie in and remain in the barn until the accomplishment of the birth. Pön also fosters tremendous reverence for the holiness and the wisdom of the old. Thus it is the grandmother who, at the first appearance of the morning star, fetches water from the brook and brings it to the mother and infant. (The morning star is believed to be the star of the forehead, which represents wisdom and learnedness. The Pön notion of the morning star also contains the idea of newness. In the Pön calendar, the change of date takes place when the morning star appears, inviting the dawn.) Once the child is born, it is identified with its family heritage—including its family mountain, family lake, and family tree. It is also assigned a turquoise stone, as the family possesses one for each of its members.

The rite associated with birth is called *lalu*, which means "ransoming the la." The word *la* is similar in meaning to the word "soul." All human beings possess a *la*; consciousness, or *sem*; and life, or *sok*. In the Pön tradition, animals do not possess a la. The la is an entity which is part of one's being but is unintelligent. Therefore it can be stolen, confiscated, or regained, as well as reinforced by spiritual power. It can be magnetized by any form of warmth or invitation. A child's la is born when the child leaves the womb and the umbilicus is cut. Butter and milk are associated with the la because of their white color, which, as already mentioned, represents goodness or divinity. In the lalu ceremony, which is still practiced, an image of a sheep is made from butter, and the infant is washed in milk, to invite the la to stay.

The lalu ceremony is also used to combat sickness. Sickness is thought by Pön believers to be caused directly or indirectly by the dégyés or by certain evil forces. It begins through the weakening of a person's vitality. This might be caused by what is called a *dön*. Döns lurk furtively outside the dominion of Yeshen and have something of a hungry-ghost or thieving-dog quality—timid, but once gaining a hold, not letting go. A dön enters the system of a person who has abused the divine order, or perhaps it enters at a moment of depression or of some other weakness. Once a person is possessed by a dön, there is an opening for a minion of one of the dégyés to steal his la. If this happens, then the *sok* (life) is subject to attack and capture by means of all kinds of sicknesses. If this attack is successful the person dies. In the case of an illness caused by the direct punishment of one of the eight dégyés, life can be taken without going through the above stages; a dégyé can take control of the sok directly. A dön or a minion of a dégyé takes a la or sok because he can use it to add to his own presence and vitality.

Healing takes different forms, depending on the cause determined for the sickness. In some cases, a ceremony against a dön can be performed. This is done by making an effigy of the sick person and offering it, along with some meat and the hair or clothes of the sick person, to the dön as a replacement. Or, if a highly accomplished priest is available, he may perform a rite to gather all the döns in the area and frighten them off by manifesting as the wrathful Se. If this succeeds, the illness ends. If it fails, the lalu ceremony, mentioned above, is performed.

In this case, the lalu ceremony is performed partly to give a ransom to the confiscator of the la, but in addition to remagnetize the la to the sick person. In order to do this, certain objects are reconsecrated: the person's turquoise stone; his la cup (a cup owned by each individual specifically for this purpose); and the thigh bone of a sheep, inscribed with the person's name and astrological chart, and wrapped with colored threads representing the five elements, with the element of the person's birth year in the center. If this is effective, the illness is cured.

If this process also fails, it is a question of a very serious illness—a matter of life and death. Then an accomplished priest must be summoned. The priest would perform the *to* rite, which invokes the power of Se and calls for the eight dégyés. The priest offers them small structures, resembling little houses fashioned out of thread, as dwelling places.

Another still weightier ceremony is called *dö*. This ceremony is often used by Buddhists in order to invoke the *gönpos*, (or *mahakalas* in Sanskrit)—the protectors. The Pön ceremony invokes the dégyé thought to be involved in the illness. In this ceremony the dégyé is offered a new castle, a very elaborate miniature construction called a *dö*. The intent of the rite is to lure the dégyé not only out of the sick person but also out of his own dwelling place. Daily offerings are made, and at the end of a certain period there is a special session in which the dö is finally and completely offered to the dégyé if he will quit the sick person.

There are further ceremonies of this nature which can be performed only by priests of the highest accomplishment. In one of these, the priest threatens to destroy the dö if the dégyé refuses to release the sick person. In a still more dire rite, the priest identifies with Se and thus with the dégyés, and, calling them, he imprisons them in certain appropriate sacred objects which he then buries. If the priest fails in the execution of this ceremony, it is considered a catastrophe since the attempt would enrage the dégyés and they would take revenge. Quite possibly the priest himself might become sick or die.

Another important Pön practice seems to be the counterclockwise circumambulation of a mountain sacred to Se and the dégyés, while performing the lhasang ritual at various points along the way.

As well, we have evidence of some incantations in the ancient Shangshung language, which there is reason to believe may have been the ancestor of the Tibetan language. These incantations are thought to develop spiritual power, especially when accompanied by certain physical movements in the form of a dance. There were also supposedly some visualizations of Pön deities meant to be combined with the incantation and dance practice, but of these we know nothing. When the practitioner has completed intensive training in these practices he demonstrates his achievement of power by throwing butter sculptures into boiling water and pulling them out again intact, or by licking heated iron.

Many aspects of the Pön religion remain to be described, but unfortunately the task greatly exceeds the scope of this short presentation. Nevertheless we hope that the outlines for an accurate picture of this religion have been sketched and some sense given of its basic nature.

The Vajrayogini Shrine

Some understanding of coemergent wisdom is necessary in order to appreciate the significance of the Vajrayogini shrine and the ritual objects that are part of it. When we begin to realize the coemergent quality of reality, we recognize that even a simple object, like a vase or a chair or a table, contains the potential power to spark wakefulness. The same is true for any sense perception or any emotion we may experience. We find ourselves in a world of self-existing messages. Because we are able to "read" the messages of the phenomenal world as statements of sacred outlook, we can properly appreciate the shrine of Vajrayogini, for the shrine embodies these self-existing messages and communicates them to others. The shrine is not set up for the worship of an external god or force; rather it is designed to focus the messages of sanity and wakefulness that exist in the world, to bring them down into the experience of the practitioner, and, in some sense, to amplify their brilliance and power.

The vajrayana has sometimes been misinterpreted as a highly symbolic system. For example, we often hear that the vajra scepter *symbolizes* skillful means or that the ghanta *symbolizes* wisdom. When it is said that the vajra is a symbol of skillful means or of indestructibility, that is true; but, in the genuine vajrayana sense, it is not simply that the vajra is used to represent or symbolize skillful means because skillful means is too abstract a concept to be dealt with, or shown, directly. The vajra scepter *is* skillful means; it actually communicates and transmits skillful action directly if one understands the literalness of the vajrayana. For that reason, the shrine of Vajrayogini and all the implements on the shrine are themselves regarded as sacred objects.

The shrine shown in the illustration is an abhisheka shrine; that is, it includes all of the objects that are used in conferring the abhisheka of Vajrayogini. A simplified version of this shrine would be used for the daily practice of the sadhana.

The mandala of Vajrayogini is placed in the center of the shrine. The mandala is traditionally made of colored sand, or sometimes it is painted. A mandala made of heaps of rice is used if neither a painted mandala nor a sand mandala can be made. The mandala and the objects above it, which will be discussed next, are regarded as a particular power spot, or focus, of the shrine for magnetizing the energy and blessings of Vajrayogini, that is, for magnetizing self-existing wakefulness.

In the center of the painted mandala one finds a symbol for the hooked knife which Vajrayogini holds in her right hand. This means that the principal yidam, Vajrayogini herself, stands at the center of the mandala. In the painted mandala, the hooked knife is situated in the middle of two crossed triangles, which represent the two *sources of dharmas* (chöjung) which are the palace and the seat of Vajrayogini. The source of dharmas that is Vajrayogini's palace is actually a three-faced pyramid (trihedron), but it is represented in the painted mandala in only two dimensions. The apex of the triangle is an infinitesimal dot that points downward; the mouth of the triangle, in which Vajrayogini stands, is vast and spacious.

The source of dharmas arises out of emptiness and has three characteristics: it is unborn, nondwelling, and unceasing. Essentially it is absolute space with a boundary or frame. This represents the coemergent quality of wisdom and confusion arising from the emptiness of space. The source of dharmas is sometimes referred to as a channel for *shunyata* or as the cosmic cervix. The source of dharmas is an abstract form of coemergence while

A TRADITIONAL VAJRAYOGINI SHRINE

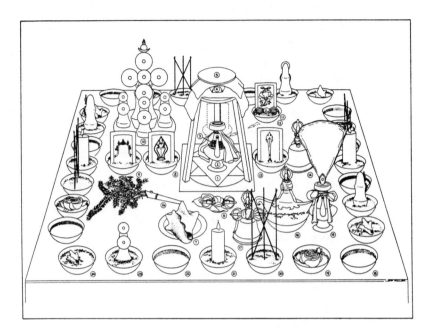

1. Mandala of Vajrayogini
2. Tsobum vase (2a: Top of tsobum vase)
3. Small vajra with five-colored thread
4. Skull cup
5. Mirror mandala
6. Vajra with white ribbon
7. Conch for oath water
8. Jewel tsakali
9. Crown tsakali
10. Phagmo torma
11. Flower tsakali
12. Vajra with red ribbon
13. Sword tsakali
14. Bell with green ribbon
15. Lebum
16. Hooked knife
17. Joined bell and dorje
18–24. Seven traditional offerings (repeated on each of the four sides):
    18. Water
    19. Flowers
    20. Incense
    21. Light
    22. Perfumed water
    23. Food (torma)
    24. Music (symbolized by small conch)

Vajrayogini is the iconographic or anthropomorphic form of the Coemergent Mother. The shape of the triangle—pointed at the bottom and wide at the top—signifies that every aspect of space can be accommodated at once—microcosm and macrocosm, the most minute situations as well as the most vast.

It is interesting that, in many theistic traditions, the pyramid is a symbol of reaching upward to unite with the godhead. The pinnacle of a pyramid or the apex of a cathedral reaches high into the clouds above. In this case, the source of dharmas reaches down, so that pleasure, pain, freedom, and imprisonment all meet at the lowest of the low points of the pyramid. In the nontheistic tradition of Buddhist tantra, the triangle reaches down and down into the ground of reality; when one reaches all the way down to the apex of the triangle, one discovers water in that ground, which is known as compassion and as amrita.

In the four cardinal points of the painted mandala, surrounding the hooked knife in the center, are the symbols of vajra, ratna, padma, and karma. Vajrayogini manifests her basic buddha family quality in the central space of the mandala. However, the energy of Vajrayogini creates a complete mandala that encompasses, or works with, the energies of all of the buddha families. Thus, in the iconography of Vajrayogini, she is surrounded by her retinue: the vajra dakini in the east, the ratna dakini in the south, the padma dakini in the west, and the karma dakini in the north. This is shown in the painted mandala by the symbols of the buddha families in the four cardinal points: the vajra in the east, representing her buddha-vajra quality; the jewel in the south, representing her buddha-ratna quality; the lotus in the west, representing her buddha-padma quality; and the sword in the north, representing her buddha-karma quality. The painted mandala also depicts coils of joy, which symbolize the mahasukha, the great bliss, that Vajrayogini confers.

On top of the mandala on the shrine is placed the chief abhisheka vase, the tsobum. During the first vase abhiseka, as discussed earlier, the practitioners are empowered with water from the tsobum. Above the painted mandala is a tripod on which is placed a skull cup filled with amrita, which is used in conferring the second abhisheka, the secret abhisheka. This transmission dissolves the student's mind into the mind of the teacher and the lineage. In general, amrita is the principle of intoxicating extreme beliefs, based on the belief in ego, and dissolving the boundary between confusion and sanity so that coemergence can be realized.

On the skull cup is placed the mirror mandala of Vajrayogini— a mirror coated with red *sindura* dust, in which is inscribed the mandala and mantra of Vajrayogini. The mirror shows that the phenomenal world reflects the wakefulness of Vajrayogini and that her mandala is reflected in the experience of the practitioner. This is the same self-existing message that was discussed earlier. The red sindura dust that covers the mirror represents the cosmic lust and passion of the Coemergent Mother. At this level of practice, passion is no longer regarded as a problem. Freed from grasping, it becomes a force of expansion and communication; it is the expression of "self-luminous compassion" as is said in the *Vajrayogini Sadhana*.

Surrounding this arrangement of the painted mandala, the abhisheka vase, the skull cup, and the mirror are objects connected with the five buddha families and used in the transmission of the abhisheka of the vase. Directly in front of the painted mandala, in the east, is placed the five-pointed vajra, the symbol of the vajra family. The symbols of the buddha family—the crossed bell and dorjé and the hooked knife—are also placed here, slightly off to one side. In the south (stage right) are placed the crown and the jewel representing the ratna family. In the west (behind the mandala) are placed the nine-pointed vajra and lotus, representing the padma family. In the north (stage left) are the ghanta and the sword, representing the karma family. If the actual objects representing the buddha families are not available, painted cards (*tsakali*) depicting the objects are placed on the shrine. A second abhisheka vase, the *lebum,* is placed in the northeast corner of the shrine. The lebum is considered to be the embodiment of the karma dakini. At the beginning of the abhisheka, prior to the abhisheka of the vase, the students drink water from the lebum to purify and cleanse themselves; at various points in the ceremony the vajra master sprinkles the disciples with water from the lebum to signify further purifying and overcoming of psychological obstacles. The conch shell, which holds the oath water of samaya, is placed in the front (east) of the shrine between the vajra family symbols and offering bowls on the edge of the shrine.

In the southern quadrant of the shrine (stage right) are also placed the *phagmo tormas,* which represent Vajrayogini and her retinue. Torma is a form of bread sculpture made from barley flour, water, alcohol, and other ingredients. The phagmo tormas on the shrine are an important means of making offerings to Vajrayogini, and in doing so, inviting the blessings of the yidam and of the lineage into the environment of practice. The tormas play a central role in the feast offering *(ganachakra),* a part of the *Vajrayogini Sadhana.* The basic idea of the feast offering is to make an offering of all sense perceptions and experience, transforming what might otherwise be expressions of confusion or indulgence into wakefulness.

On the edges of the shrine box are four sets of offering bowls, seven bowls to a set. The seven offerings are: saffron water, flowers, incense, lamps, food, perfumed water, and musical instruments. The offering of saffron water represents cleansing neurotic tendencies and emotional defilements, or *kleshas,* of body, speech, and mind. As is said in the sadhana:

> In order to cleanse the klesha tendencies of sentient
> beings
> We offer this ablution water for body, speech, and
> mind.

The offering of flowers represents offerings of pleasing sense perceptions:

> Flowers pleasing to the victorious ones of all mandalas
> Superior, well-formed, celestial varieties.

The offering of incense represents discipline:

> The fragrance of discipline is the best supreme incense.

The offering of lamps represents prajna:

> Burning the poisonous kleshas and dispelling the
> darkness of ignorance,
> The brilliance of prajna is a glorious torch.

The offering of perfumed water represents kindness:

> Pure water mixed with perfume and herbal ingredients
> is the bathing water of the victorious ones. . . .
> May kindness, raining continually from cloudbanks of
> wisdom, purify the multitude of foul odors.

The offering of food represents amrita:

> Though the victorious ones have no hunger,
> For the benefit of beings we offer this divine amrita
> food.

The offering of musical instruments represents the melody of liberation:

> The gong and cymbals are the liberating melody of
> Brahma.

On the wall behind the shrine or on an adjacent wall is a *thangka,* or painting, of Vajrayogini. The thangka of vajrayana is further tribute to her, and it is also on aid to visualization for the practitioner.

List of Sources

CHAPTER 1   What Is the Heart of the Buddha?
Vajradhatu Sun 4 no. 3 (February/March 1981).

CHAPTER 2   Intellect and Intuition
Previously unpublished.

CHAPTER 3   The Four Foundations of Mindfulness
Garuda IV, Boulder: Vajradhatu Publications (1976).

CHAPTER 4   Devotion
Empowerment, Boulder: Vajradhatu Publications (1976).

CHAPTER 5   Taking Refuge
Garuda V, Boulder: Vajradhatu Publications (1977).

CHAPTER 6   The Bodhisattva Vow
Garuda V, Boulder: Vajradhatu Publications (1977).

CHAPTER 7   Sacred Outlook: The Practice of Vajrayogini
"Sacred Outlook: The Vajrayogini Shrine and Practice." *The Silk Route and the Diamond Path: Esoteric Buddhist Art on the Trade Routes of the Trans-Himalayan Region*, Dr. Deborah Klimburg-Salter, ed., Los Angeles: UCLA Art Council Press (1977).

CHAPTER 8   Relationship
Maitreya 5: Relationship, Berkeley: Shambhala Publications (1974).

CHAPTER 9   Acknowledging Death
Journal of Contemplative Psychotherapy 3, Boulder: The Naropa Institute (1982). (First published in *Healing,* Olsen and Fossaghe, eds., New York: Human Sciences Press, 1978.)

CHAPTER 10   Alcohol as Medicine or Poison
"Amrita as Poison or Medicine." *Vajradhatu Sun* 2 no. 3 (February/March 1980).

CHAPTER 11   Practice and Basic Goodness: A Talk for Children
"Talk by the Vajracarya to the Childrens' Program." *Vajradhatu Sun* 1 no. 5 (June/July 1979).

CHAPTER 12   Dharma Poetics
"Vajracarya on Dharma Poetics." *Vajradhatu Sun* 5 no. 2 (December 1982/January 1983).

CHAPTER 13   Green Energy
Harper's Magazine (November 1973).

CHAPTER 14   Manifesting Enlightenment
Vajradhatu Sun 6 no. 1 (October/November 1983).

The Pön Way of Life
Vajradhatu Sun 7 no. 2 (December 1984/January 1985).

The Vajrayogini Shrine
"Sacred Outlook: The Vajrayogini Shrine and Practice." *The Silk Route and the Diamond Path: Esoteric Buddhist Art on the Trade Routes of the Trans-Himalayan Region,* Dr. Deborah Klimburg-Salter, ed., Los Angeles: UCLA Art Council Press (1977).

About the Author

Ven. Chögyam Trungpa was born in the province of Kham in Eastern Tibet, in 1940. When he was just thirteen months old, Chögyam Trungpa was recognized as a major *tülku,* or incarnate teacher. According to Tibetan tradition, an enlightened teacher is capable, based on his or her vow of compassion, of reincarnating in human form over a succession of generations. Before dying, such a teacher leaves a letter or other clue to the whereabouts of the next incarnation. Later, students and other realized teachers look through these clues and, based on careful examination of dreams and visions, conduct searches to discover and recognize the successor. Thus, particular lines of teaching are formed, in some cases extending over several centuries. Chögyam Trungpa was the eleventh in the teaching lineage known as the Trungpa Tülkus.

Once young tülkus are recognized, they enter a period of intensive training in the theory and practice of the Buddhist teachings. Trungpa Rinpoche (*Rinpoche* is an honorific title meaning "precious one"), after being enthroned as supreme abbot of Surmang Monasteries and governor of Surmang District, began a period of training that would last eighteen years, until his departure from Tibet in 1959. As a Kagyü tülku, his training was based on the systematic practice of meditation and on refined theoretical understanding of Buddhist philosophy. One of the four great lineages of Tibet, the Kagyü is known as the "practice lineage."

At the age of eight, Trungpa Rinpoche received ordination as a novice monk. After his ordination, he engaged in intensive study and practice of the traditional monastic disciplines as well as in the arts of calligraphy, thangka painting, and monastic dance. His primary teachers were Jamgön Kongtrül of Sechen and Khenpo Kangshar—leading teachers in the Nyingma and Kagyü lineages. In 1958, at the age of eighteen, Trungpa Rinpoche completed his studies, receiving the degree of *kyorpön* (doctor of divinity) and *khenpo* (master of studies). He also received full monastic ordination.

The late fifties were a time of great upheaval in Tibet. As it became clear that the Chinese Communists intended to take over the country by force, many people, both monastic and lay, fled the country. Trungpa Rinpoche spent many harrowing months trekking over the Himalayas (described in his book *Born in Tibet*). After narrowly escaping capture by the Chinese, he at last reached India in 1959. While in India, Trungpa Rinpoche was appointed by His Holiness Tenzin Gyatso, the fourteenth Dalai Lama, to serve as spiritual advisor to the Young Lamas Home School in Dalhousie, India. He served in this capacity from 1959 to 1963.

Trungpa Rinpoche's first opportunity to encounter the West came when he received a Spaulding sponsorship to attend Oxford University. At Oxford he studied comparative religion, philosophy, and fine arts. He also studied Japanese flower arranging, receiving a degree from the Sogetsu School. While in England, Trungpa Rinpoche began to instruct Western students in the *dharma* (the teachings of the Buddha), and in 1968 he founded, along with Akong Tulku, the Samye Ling Meditation Centre in Dumfriesshire, Scotland. During this period he also published two books, both in English: *Born in Tibet* and *Meditation in Action*.

In 1969, Trungpa Rinpoche traveled to Bhutan, where he entered into a solitary meditation retreat. This retreat marked a pivotal change in his approach to teaching. Immediately upon returning he became a lay person, putting aside his monastic robes and dressing in ordinary Western attire. He also married a young English woman, and together they left Scotland and moved to

North America. Many of his early students found these changes shocking and upsetting. However, he expressed a conviction that, in order to take root in the West, the dharma needed to be taught free from cultural trappings and religious fascination. During the seventies America was in a period of political and cultural ferment. It was a time of fascination with the East. Trungpa Rinpoche criticized the materialistic and commercialized approach to spirituality he encountered, describing it as a "spiritual supermarket." In his lectures, and in his books *Cutting Through Spiritual Materialism* and *The Myth of Freedom,* he pointed to the simplicity and directness of the practice of sitting meditation as the way to cut through such distortions of the spiritual journey.

During his seventeen years of teaching in North America, Trungpa Rinpoche developed a reputation as a dynamic and controversial teacher. Fluent in the English language, he was one of the first *lamas* who could speak to Western students directly, without the aid of a translator. Traveling extensively throughout North America and Europe, Trungpa Rinpoche gave hundreds of talks and seminars. He established major centers in Vermont, Colorado, and Nova Scotia, as well as many smaller meditation and study centers in cities throughout North America and Europe. Vajradhatu was formed in 1973 as the central administrative body of this network.

In 1974, Trungpa Rinpoche founded the Naropa Institute, which became the only accredited Buddhist-inspired university in North America. He lectured extensively at the Institute, and his book *Journey Without Goal* is based on a course he taught there. In 1976, he established the Shambhala Training program, a series of weekend programs and seminars which provides instruction in meditation practice within a secular setting. His book *Shambhala: The Sacred Path of the Warrior* gives an overview of the Shambhala teachings.

Trungpa Rinpoche was also active in the field of translation. Working with Francesca Fremantle, he rendered a new translation of *The Tibetan Book of the Dead,* which was published in 1975.

Later he formed the Nalanda Translation Committee, in order to translate texts and liturgies for his own students as well as to make important texts available publicly.

Trungpa Rinpoche was also known for his interest in the arts, and particularly for his insights into the relationship between contemplative discipline and the artistic process. His own art work included calligraphy, painting, flower arranging, poetry, playwriting, and environmental installations. In addition, at the Naropa Institute, he created an educational atmosphere which attracted many leading artists and poets. The exploration of the creative process in light of contemplative training continues there as a provocative dialogue. Trungpa Rinpoche has published two books of poetry: *Mudra* and *First Thought Best Thought*.

During his seventeen years of teaching in North America, he crafted the structures necessary to provide his students with thorough, systematic training in the dharma. From introductory talks and courses to advanced group retreat practices, these programs emphasize a balance of study and practice, of intellect and intuition. Students at all levels can pursue their interest in meditation and the Buddhist path through these many forms of training. Senior students of Trungpa Rinpoche are involved in both teaching and meditation instruction in such programs. In addition to his extensive teachings in the Buddhist tradition, Trungpa Rinpoche also placed great emphasis on the Shambhala teachings, which stress the importance of mind-training, as distinct from religious practice; community involvement and the creation of an enlightened society; and appreciation of one's day-to-day life.

Trungpa Rinpoche passed away in 1987, at the age of forty-seven. He is survived by his wife, Diana, and five sons. By the time of his death, Trungpa Rinpoche had become known as a pivotal figure in introducing dharma to the Western world. The joining of his great appreciation for Western culture and his deep understanding of his own tradition led to a revolutionary approach to teaching the dharma, in which the most ancient and profound teachings were presented in a thoroughly contemporary way.

Trungpa Rinpoche was known for his fearless proclamation of the dharma: free from hesitation, true to the purity of the tradition, and utterly fresh. May these teachings take root and flourish for the benefit of all sentient beings.

Index

Italicized page numbers refer to illustrations.

258 • INDEX

BOOKS BY CHÖGYAM TRUNGPA

The Art of Calligraphy: Joining Heaven and Earth
Born in Tibet
Crazy Wisdom
Cutting Through Spiritual Materialism
The Dawn of Tantra
   by Herbert V. Guenther and Chögyam Trungpa
Dharma Art
First Thought Best Thought: 108 Poems
Glimpses of Abhidharma
The Heart of the Buddha
Illusion's Game: The Life and Teaching of Naropa
Journey without Goal: The Tantric Wisdom of the Buddha
The Life of Marpa the Translator
   Translated by the Nālandā Translation Committee under the
     direction of Chögyam Trungpa
The Lion's Roar: An Introduction to Tantra
Meditation in Action
Mudra
The Myth of Freedom and the Way of Meditation
Orderly Chaos: The Mandala Principle
The Path Is the Goal: A Basic Handbook of Buddhist Meditation
The Rain of Wisdom: The Essence of the Ocean of True Meaning
   Translated by the Nālandā Translation Committee under the
     direction of Chögyam Trungpa
Shambhala: The Sacred Path of the Warrior
The Tibetan Book of the Dead: The Great Liberation through
   Hearing in the Bardo
   Translated with commentary by Francesca Fremantle and
     Chögyam Trungpa
Training the Mind and Cultivating Loving-Kindness
Transcending Madness: The Experience of the Six Bardos